PENGUIN PASSNOTES

Lord of the Flies

Gillian Hanscombe, D.Phil. (Oxon), was born in Australia and was educated at the Universities of Melbourne, Monash and Oxford. She also has a Post Graduate Certificate of Education from London University. Having taught in schools for a period, she then became a journalist and freelance writer, specializing in educational writing.

PENGUIN PASSNOTES

WILLIAM GOLDING
Lord of the Flies

G. HANSCOMBE, M.A., CERT.ED., D.PHIL.
ADVISORY EDITOR: STEPHEN COOTE, M.A., PH.D.

PENGUIN BOOKS

Penguin Books Ltd, Harmondsworth, Middlesex, England
Viking Penguin Inc., 40 West 23rd Street, New York, New York 10010, U.S.A.
Penguin Books Australia Ltd, Ringwood, Victoria, Australia
Penguin Books Canada Ltd, 2801 John Street, Markham, Ontario, Canada L3R 1B4
Penguin Books (N.Z.) Ltd, 182-190 Wairau Road, Auckland 10, New Zealand

First published 1986
Reprinted 1986, 1987

Interactive approach developed by Susan Quilliam

Page references in this book refer to the trade edition of *Lord of the Flies*
published by Faber & Faber
The publishers are grateful to the *Observer* newspaper for permission to
reproduce the story on p. 69

Made and printed in Great Britain by
Richard Clay Ltd, Bungay, Suffolk
Filmset in Monophoto Ehrhardt

Contents

To the Student

The purpose of this book is to help you appreciate William Golding's novel *Lord of the Flies*. It will help you to understand details of the plot. It will also help you to think about the characters, about what the writer is trying to say and how he says it. These things are most important. After all, understanding and responding to plots, characters and ideas are what make books come alive for us.

You will find this Passnote most useful after you have read *Lord of the Flies* through at least once. A first reading will reveal the plot and make you think about the lives of the people it describes and your feelings for them. Now your job will be to make those first impressions clear. You will need to read the book again and ask yourself some questions. What does the writer really mean? What do I think about this incident or that one? How does the writer make such-and-such a character come alive?

This Passnote has been designed to help you do this. It offers you background information. It also asks many questions. You may like to write answers to some of these. Others you can answer in your head. The questions are meant to make you think, feel and respond. As you answer them, you will gain a clearer knowledge of the book and of your own ideas about it. When your thoughts are indeed clear, then you will be able to write confidently because you have made yourself an alert and responsive reader.

Introduction

Lord of the Flies is sometimes described as William Golding's first novel. It was his first *published* novel, so in one way it is true to say it is his first. What people may not know is that he wrote three others before this one, none of which was accepted by the many publishers he sent them to.

It is important to know about how a writer fails, as well as how he or she succeeds. Such information tells us a lot about how writers try first this way and then that way to speak to their unknown audience, to the public, to you and me. Sometimes the writer finds that people do not specially like the story he or she is telling; at other times people do not like the way the story is told. Everyone has favourite stories which they recommend to other people. *Lord of the Flies* has become one of these ever since it was first published in 1954. It has sold well over eleven million copies in its three decades of publication.

When a writer produces three novels which no one wants, and then one which a vast number of people very much want, we become intrigued. How did he come to write this particular story?

In a television interview given after he had won the Nobel Prize for Literature – which is the most famous international prize a writer can win – William Golding explained some of the circumstances in which he wrote this novel. He was earning his living as a teacher of English and classics in a school near Salisbury, in the south of England. He and his wife took turns each evening to read to their young children, and they were embarked upon reading Victorian Island stories (*Treasure Island* and *The Coral Island* are two you may have read or heard about). After finishing a particular episode, Golding said to his wife one night that it would be fun to write a book about what actually *would* happen to children stranded on an island. He meant, by saying this, that although the Victorian stories were exciting, he did not really believe that children – nor any other people in this situation – would simply have fun and adventures and would be sensible and well-meaning. He meant that it would be interesting to write a story in which the people on the island behaved in ways that showed us what human nature is really like; that, among other things, it is capable of great evil.

With his wife's encouragement, Golding set about writing such a story. The whole book was in his mind from the beginning, so – at the rate of 2,000 words a day – he wrote out what was already in his head. The writing of the book took about six weeks. It was 1952.

Remember that in the early 1950s the Second World War was a recent experience for everyone. William Golding had been a young man during the war and had served in the Royal Navy. He became persuaded that Nazism – the philosophy of Hitler and his followers, who established the German Third Reich – was an absolute evil. The practice of Nazism changed his view of what people are like. He began to think that human beings have an immense capacity for evil. That is why he thought that boys left alone on an island would express that capacity for evil, rather than just the reasonableness which people are taught to believe is uppermost in our behaviour with one another.

Golding owed his earlier views – as we all mainly do – to his background. He was brought up in Wiltshire by radical parents, people who challenged the political system around them. His father was a socialist and rationalist; his mother had been a suffragette. In other words, they believed in the state owning important factories, in reason and in women having the vote. Consequently, Golding was made aware from an early age of social differences and how they are enforced. But there was something else in his temperament which he did not share with his father: an instinct for the supernatural. He recalls arguing passionately with his father about the nature of things. His father held to scientific views, which hold that everything can be explained through intelligence, while the young Golding argued for the supernatural. That is one reason why he came to see Nazism as an evil force, rather than as merely a bad political system. The evil of Nazism could not be explained through reason alone. He says that *Lord of the Flies* takes the supposed innocent experience of island-like life – the life depicted in the novels he read to his own children – in order to test it against the experience of Nazism and the Second World War.

This does not mean that Golding wrote his novel as an exact parallel of the war. He wanted it to discuss some of the issues the war had raised.

He also says that what really interests him is exploring 'what gives power to a story'. He means that he does not want just to tell what happens, but to tell what happens in a way that will examine and explain *why* and *how* it happens.

While you are reading Golding's story, there will be things you should think carefully about. Who are the people in the story, and what are they like? Why does it take place where it does? What actually happens? Why do the people do the things they do? Finally you should ask the most important question of all: what is the point of this story?

As you discover the answers to these and other questions, you will know what you think of the story – whether it is worth reading or not and whether Golding has told it well or not.

There are many different ways to tell a story. You can put some things in and leave others out; you can make some things much more important than other things; you can make people laugh at something or make them think very seriously about it. You can find this out for yourself by telling a story about a place you have seen, a person you have met, something you have done. You can try writing down the same story; and then you can try writing it quite differently. You will see, if you do, what Golding is talking about when he says what interests him is what there is in a story that makes it convincing.

As we read *Lord of the Flies* together, we shall consider the story's *plot*: the incidents and events that happen, in the order in which they happen. This is what you will find in the 'Summary' section. Then we shall look at *how the story is told*: which circumstances, conversations, thoughts, feelings and observations Golding thinks we should know. This is what you will find in the 'Commentary' section. After that, we shall consider the main characters in the story: what kinds of choices they have and what decisions they make. This is what you will find the 'Characters' section is about. Following that, we shall think about the *point* of the story, *why* it is being told to us. This is what the 'Themes' section is about. We shall read some writing by other people in the 'Passages for Comparison' section; and finally, in the 'Glossary', you will find explained some of the more unusual words Golding uses in his story.

Lord of the Flies is what some people call a 'story with a message'. You will find it fascinating to follow and examine how the telling of the story contains the message Golding wishes to teach. People see things differently and you may find, in the end, that your conclusions are different from Golding's. You may find, on the other hand, that things you were half-aware of are sharpened into direct focus for you. But whatever conclusions we come to, we know that reading and listening to stories does – in some ways – change us.

Summary

CHAPTER 1, *pp. 7–34*

The story begins in hot jungle, with a fair-haired boy in school uniform clambering among creepers and fallen tree trunks. We are not told his name straight away, nor what the 'long scar smashed into the jungle' is (p. 7). Another boy calls to the first. This boy is shorter, very fat and wears glasses (p. 7).

As they begin talking, we become aware that they have been in an aeroplane that caught fire (p. 8). The fair boy is keen to explore where they are. He thinks they may be on an island and that there may be no grown-ups with them (p. 8). The fat boy latches on to the fair boy and finds out that his name is Ralph; but Ralph is not interested in learning his companion's name (p. 9). He presses on towards the beach and takes off his clothes. We learn that he is just over twelve years old (p. 10).

The fat boy follows and tries again to make conversation; but the only thing that interests Ralph is the fat boy's nickname: Piggy (p. 11). He shrieks with laughter, despite Piggy's protests that he doesn't want this name. Piggy pleads with Ralph not to tell it to anyone else (p. 12).

Ralph swims in a warm pool (p. 13). Piggy has never learned to swim, because of his asthma (p. 14), but he takes off his clothes and sits in the water. Ralph says his father, who is in the navy, will come and rescue them (p. 14). Piggy has no parents, but has lived with his 'auntie'; and anyway, he doubts Ralph's claim, reminding him that the pilot had told them there had been an atom-bomb blast (p. 14). Both boys consider the possibility that everyone they know might be dead (p. 15).

Ralph notices a huge shell in the waters of the lagoon (p. 16). Piggy says it is called a conch and that you can blow it like a trumpet (p. 16). Ralph takes it from the water and blows it (pp. 17–18). As a result, other boys appear, one by one (pp. 18–19), and Piggy begins to take their names. They are wearing different school uniforms (p. 19), except for a long black column of boys wearing robes and strange hats, who march along in pairs (p. 20). They are members of a choir (p. 21) and their leader wants to be called by his last name, Merridew, rather than his first name, Jack, which he calls a 'kid's name'. Ralph cruelly tells everyone that the fat boy is called Piggy.

They decide to vote for a leader and choose Ralph, rather than Jack, for chief (p. 24). Ralph declares that Jack may remain in charge of his choir (p. 25) and that three of the group should explore their surroundings (p. 25). He chooses Jack and Simon to go with him (pp. 25–6). Piggy follows, hurt that Ralph has told everyone his nickname (p. 26). Ralph instructs him to go back to the others and take their names (p. 27). The others begin exploring (pp. 27–30). They climb to the top of a high hill and see that they are on an island (p. 31). They decide it must be uninhabited (p. 32). On their way down they see a wild piglet (p. 33). Jack draws his knife to kill it, but while he hesitates the animal escapes (p. 33).

CHAPTER 2, *pp. 35–51*

After returning from exploring the island, Ralph blows the conch to call the second meeting (p. 35). He explains what they have discovered, and Jack adds that despite the island being uninhabited, they need an army to hunt the wild pigs they have seen (p. 35).

Ralph wants the group to understand that not everyone can speak at once. When a boy wants to speak, he should put up his hand, like at school, and he will be given the conch (p. 36). Anyone holding the conch will not be interrupted, except by Ralph himself. Piggy explains that no one knows where they are and Ralph adds that they may be stuck there for a long time (p. 38). He points out, nevertheless, that there is plenty of food and bathing-water and that they can all have a good time. A small six-year-old tells Ralph he is afraid of 'the snake-thing', which he calls 'a beastie' (p. 39). Ralph assures him that such things would only be found in a big country like Africa or India, not on an island (p. 39). He then tells them they must light a fire to help anyone looking for them to know where they are (p. 41). Everyone except Piggy rushes off to start building one. They take Piggy's glasses, using its lenses and the sun, to ignite the fire, after realizing that no one has any matches (p. 44). Jack says his hunters – the choir – will keep it going (p. 47).

The fire spreads by itself. Everyone except Piggy is excited by the huge flames (p. 49). Piggy says they ought to have made shelters first (p. 50). He points out, too, that one tiny boy is missing, so they should not have made such an uncontrollable fire without thinking what it might do (p. 51).

CHAPTER 3, *pp. 52–62*

Jack, naked except for his shorts and knife-belt, and carrying a spear he has made , is hunting pigs, while Ralph and the others build shelters on the beach (pp. 52–4). Ralph is exasperated with the younger boys, who are called 'littluns', because they keep running off to play and swim (pp. 54–5). He wants the shelters finished, not only for protection from sun and rain but also because the littluns are frightened at night and suffer from bad dreams (p. 56). Ralph explains that they need the shelters as a home. But Jack is possessed by a passion for hunting, for killing and for meat (pp. 56–7). Ralph and Jack irritate each other and are unable to understand each other's obsessions (pp. 58–9).

While Ralph and Jack walk off to find the others in the bathing-pool, Simon slips away alone into the jungle (p. 60). He finds a natural hiding-place, creeps into it and watches the evening fall, listening intently to the cries of birds and insects, and to the sound of the sea (pp. 61–2).

CHAPTER 4, *pp. 63–82*

A separation between littluns and biguns appears (p. 64). The littluns are content to play in between meetings called by the conch and doing what the biguns command (p. 65). Jack, preoccupied with his lack of success in hunting, has a new idea. He finds red and white clay, and charcoal, to paint himself with, explaining to the others that he thinks the pigs can see him too easily and that they will be deceived by the camouflage if he paints away his skin colour (p. 68). When he finishes painting himself, he begins dancing, and his laugh becomes a blood-thirsty snarling (p. 69).

Meanwhile, Ralph, Piggy, Simon and Maurice see a ship pass along the horizon (p. 71). Agonized because he cannot be sure their fire is sending a clear smoke signal, Ralph pushes through the jungle and up the hill to check their fire (pp. 72–3). The others follow. They see that the fire is dead and realize that the ship will pass on without anyone on it being provoked into searching their island (p. 74). Their chance of rescue has come and gone.

They see Jack and his choir, nearly naked, appear in procession. They are chanting. The twins, Sam and Eric, are carrying a dead pig on a stake, its throat cut (p. 74). The choir is chanting 'Kill the pig. Cut her throat. Spill her blood' (p. 75). When they meet, Ralph reproaches Jack furiously for letting the fire go out (p. 75). The others, including Piggy, agree (p. 77). Jack, humiliated, hits Piggy in the stomach (p. 77). Piggy's glasses fly off and Simon rescues them, but one lens is broken (p. 78). Jack brings himself to apologize to Ralph for letting the fire go out (p. 78). Ralph, however, is still furious and does not forgive him. He insists that Jack and his choir light the fire again (p. 79). They begin to cook the pig-meat. When Piggy asks for some, Jack taunts him. Quickly, Simon gives his own piece to Piggy. Deflated, Jack angrily gives another piece to Simon (p. 80). Jack and the choir begin to tell and re-enact how they killed the pig (p. 81). Ralph says he is going to call a meeting down on the beach (p. 82).

CHAPTER 5, *pp. 83–103*

Everyone assembles for the meeting and Ralph explains that they must put things straight (p. 86). He says they must keep the rules they make and that they must tackle the fear they all sometimes feel (p. 89). Ralph and Jack both insist to the others that there is no beast on the island (pp. 90–91). Piggy adds that there is not only no beast but no fear either, except for fear of other people (p. 92). A littlun called Phil tells the others he saw something moving in the trees at night (p. 92). The others tell him it was a dream, but he insists he was awake (p. 93). Simon admits that he has been out alone at night, wanting to go to a place he knows (p. 93). Percival, another littlun, then says the beast comes out of the sea (p. 96). Simon says that perhaps the beast is themselves, but everyone laughs at him (p. 97).

They all argue until Jack snatches the conch and shouts at Ralph that the rules do not matter (p. 100). Jack and his followers rush off down the beach, shouting and re-enacting the hunt (p. 100). Ralph, Piggy and Simon wonder what to do (p. 101). Ralph says he should give up being chief, but Piggy begs him not to (p. 102).

CHAPTER 6, *pp. 104–19*

While the boys sleep, a man drops by parachute from the distant air battle raging miles above the island (p. 104). The man is dead. The wind, by filling his parachute, drags his body to the mountain-top (p. 105). Sam and Eric, on fire duty, catch sight of the dead man's head and chest (p. 107). They rush to wake Ralph and Piggy, babbling that they have seen the beast (p. 108). Ralph calls a meeting and the twins tell their story again (p. 109). They insist that the beast has claws and wings and that it followed them (p. 109).

Jack calls the others to a hunt (p. 110). Ralph disagrees. He persuades the others to his point of view by insisting that their main priority is the fire, which Sam and Eric must have let die and which now must be lit again (p. 112). They agree that Piggy should stay with the littluns while Ralph, Jack and the biguns go to search out the beast and to re-start the fire (p. 112). Simon cannot believe the beast is anything but human (p. 113).

Ralph, despite his own fear, goes first to explore the narrow rock ledge which they think may house the beast (pp. 114–15). Jack joins them, exclaiming that the place is a perfect natural fort (p. 116). Having found no beast, they return to the others and prepare to climb the mountain to restart the fire (p. 117). A group of boys push a huge rock into the sea, and Ralph scolds them, saying the fire is the most important priority and that they shouldn't waste time on useless activities (p. 118). There is disagreement. Some want to stay and play, others to go back to the beach (p. 118). Ralph shouts at them again that they need to make the fire (p. 119).

CHAPTER 7, *pp. 120–36*

After a meal of fruit (p. 121), Ralph is feeling hopeless and looking out to sea when Simon seems to read his thoughts and tells him he thinks Ralph will get back to where he has come from (p. 122). Ralph daydreams about his home (pp. 123–4), and is brought back to reality by the sound and sight of a boar rushing at him. He takes aim with his wooden spear and throws it, wounding the animal on the snout (p. 124). The others admire him and they all begin to pretend to hunt, with Robert acting as the boar. The frenzy of the others frightens Robert (p. 126).

They set out again for the mountain (p. 128). Simon offers to cross the island alone to tell Piggy that the others will not be back until after dark (p. 129). Jack, Ralph and Roger set off for the mountain-top (p. 132). Jack does the final stage alone (p. 133). He comes back to tell Ralph and Roger that he has seen a 'thing' (p. 134). They go with Jack and all three flee from the sight that greets them: 'Something like a great ape' stares at them, and it has a ruined face (p. 136).

CHAPTER 8, *pp. 137–59*

Ralph tells Piggy, who can hardly believe him, that they've seen the beast and that it has teeth and big black eyes (p. 137). Jack calls a meeting (p. 138), telling the others about the beast and accusing Ralph of not being a proper chief (p. 139). He asks the others to vote against Ralph, but he fails to persuade them (p. 140). Jack says then that he will not be part of Ralph's group any more and will go off by himself. Anyone who wants to hunt with him can join him (p. 141).

At Piggy's suggestion, the others begin to build a new fire, this time on the beach, close to the shelters (p. 143). After a while, Ralph notices that many of the others have crept away to join Jack (p. 145). Jack happily organizes his followers to hunt pigs (p. 147). They attack and chase a sow (pp. 148–9), finally killing her (p. 149). Roger, addressing Jack as 'chief', asks how they are to make a fire to cook the meat (p. 150). Jack replies that they will raid the others and steal some fire (p. 150). He stakes the sow's head into a rock as a gift for the beast (p. 151). Ralph, meanwhile, is questioning Piggy about why no one else understands how essential the fire is (p. 154). Suddenly, painted hunters leap at them and take some burning branches (p. 154). Jack invites anyone who wishes to come and feast with him and his tribe (p. 155).

Ralph explains to those who stay that they must make smoke if they want to be rescued (p. 157). Simon, sitting alone in the jungle, realizes that the beast cannot be hunted and killed because it is part of themselves (p. 158). He feels one of his fits coming on (p. 158).

CHAPTER 9, *pp. 160–70*

Simon wakes from his fit and walks to the mountain-top. He discovers and examines the parachute and the dead body it holds (p. 160–61). Meanwhile, Ralph and Piggy – who are now alone – decide to go to Jack's feast (p. 163) and to join in the eating of meat (pp. 164–5). Jack and Ralph argue about who is now chief (p. 166), while a violent tropical storm breaks (p. 167). Jack commands the others to do their hunting dance, which they perform with Roger acting as the pig (p. 167). Simon stumbles out of the forest into the screaming circle, trying to tell them about the dead man on the mountain-top (p. 168). But the others, mad with frenzy, fall upon him and kill him (p. 169). Later, his dead body floats on the tide out to sea (p. 170).

CHAPTER 10, *pp. 171–86*

Ralph and Piggy discuss the murder of Simon (pp. 171–2). Piggy insists that it was an accident (p. 173). When they are joined by Sam and Eric, all four reassure each other that they left the feast early, though each boy knows that they all shared in the dance and the ritual that killed Simon (p. 175).

Roger finds Jack's followers in the rock fort at the end of the island (p. 176) where Jack is preparing for another hunt (p. 177). Ralph, Piggy, Sam and Eric do their best to keep their fire going (pp. 180–81), but eventually give up and go to bed in the shelters (p. 181). They hear something moving outside (p. 183). It calls for Piggy (p. 184), whose fear brings on an attack of asthma. Ralph and the attackers fight (p. 184). Along the beach, Jack and two of his tribe gloat over the broken glasses they have stolen from Piggy (p. 186).

CHAPTER 11, *pp. 187–201*

Ralph, Piggy, Sam and Eric try unsuccessfully to start their fire from its ashes (p. 187). Ralph blows the conch for a meeting (p. 188). Piggy says he will go with the conch to Jack to demand his glasses back (p. 189). The others say they will go with him (p. 190). When the four arrive at the rock fort, the tribe – all painted – demand that they say who they are. Ralph tells them not to be silly and blows the conch (p. 193). He then asks for Piggy's glasses (p. 194). They laugh at him (p. 195). Jack appears with another dead sow and tells Ralph to keep to his end of the island (p. 195). Ralph calls Jack a thief (p. 195). Jack stabs with his spear at Ralph, and Ralph parries and jabs in turn (p. 196).

Ralph tells everyone that they have come for Piggy's glasses and to remind them all of the importance of keeping a fire alight (p. 197). Jack is unmoved. He orders his tribe to grab Sam and Eric (p. 198). Ralph and Jack fight (p. 198). Piggy holds up the conch and everyone falls silent to see what he will say that they can laugh at (p. 199). Piggy asks whether they prefer to be savages or to be civilized (p. 199). Roger releases an enormous rock, which falls on Piggy, shattering the conch and hurling Piggy on to the rocks below. Piggy's skull is smashed instantly, and his dead body disappears into the sea (p. 200). The others attack Ralph with spears (p. 201). Ralph runs for his life (p. 201).

CHAPTER 12, *pp. 202–23*

Ralph, fearing for his life, waits and hides (p. 202). He searches for fruit when he knows the others are busy feasting (p. 203). When he comes across the pig's skull staked in the ground, he bashes it to pieces (p. 204).

He realizes Sam and Eric have been forced to join the tribe (p. 206). He goes to them, even so. They tell him that Jack is organizing the tribe to hunt Ralph down (pp. 207–8). They beg Ralph to go, and Sam gives him a piece of meat (p. 209). The twins tell Ralph that Roger has sharpened a stake in preparation for the hunt (p. 210). Ralph tells Sam and Eric where he will hide, asking them to lead the hunt away from his hiding-place. He crawls into his chosen hideaway and sleeps (p. 211).

Upon waking, Ralph realizes that the twins have been forced to tell Jack where Ralph is (p. 212). A huge rock is hurled towards Ralph's hideaway (p. 213). A spear thrusts in at Ralph, who thrusts back, hearing a wounded cry (p. 214). Ralph runs, gradually understanding that the tribe has set the island on fire in order to smoke him out (p. 217). He hides again (p. 218) and, when he is found, he screams and charges (p. 220). He runs frantically to the beach and falls (p. 221). He looks up to see a naval officer standing on the sand (p. 221). Ralph tells him that two boys are dead (p. 222). The others stand silently while he answers the officer's questions (p. 222). Ralph weeps (p. 223).

Commentary

CHAPTER 1, *pp. 7–34*

The very first paragraph of the story introduces us to a fair-haired boy scrambling through jungle. Immediately the writer makes us sense how hot it is. Note down the words and ideas on the first page of the book which make clear what the heat is like. One idea you will have noticed is that the boy has taken off his school sweater. Why would a boy wear a sweater in a jungle? Something unusual must have happened. Why do you think the writer does not tell us at the very beginning what has led to the boy finding himself in a jungle? Does it make you more curious, or less curious, to read on and try to find out what has happened? Why do you think so?

As well as telling us about the heat, the writer wants to tell us what the place is like. Is it flat or hilly? Are there many plants or only a few? Is it easy or difficult to walk about? Jot down on half a page of your notebook how you know what the place is like.

There is a 'scar' smashed into the jungle. What do you think it is? If you're not sure, read pages 8 and 31 again. Do you find that not knowing at the start about the plane crash makes the story more interesting? Why do you think so?

The same thing happens with regard to the boys' names. We learn them gradually. Tell someone else who is reading this book whose name we learn first and how we learn it.

Why do you think Ralph is not eager to know Piggy's name? What interests him more? When Ralph blows the conch and more boys appear, who is the most interested to know all their names? You will have realized it is Piggy. Jack, like Piggy, does not want to be known by his familiar name. He calls it a 'kid's name'. What do you think he means? Why does he prefer his surname, Merridew?

Do you like your familiar name? Why? What difference does it make to you what you are called? How does it feel different to call someone you know well by another name? Names are very important at the beginning of this story. Are they as important to you? Think about being in a crowd of strangers, where you do not know anyone's name and no one knows yours. How do you feel? Write down on a page of your notebook how your feelings change as you begin to exchange names with the others in the crowd.

At the start of the book the boys we meet first are Ralph and Piggy. What is Ralph like? What is Piggy like? Jot down a paragraph each about these two characters.

What have you remembered about them? Now go back and read pages 7–17 again. Have you left out anything important? You will have noticed, for example, that Ralph is well-built and a good swimmer, while Piggy is fat and short-sighted; and you will have noticed that Piggy suffers from asthma. What is asthma? Do you feel sorry for Piggy?

Which boy most wants to make friends with the other? If you were with them on the island, would you want to make friends with Piggy? Would you want to make friends with Ralph? Note down some of your reasons. Now note down which boy you would rather make friends with. Why do you prefer him?

Towards the end of the chapter we meet Jack. What is he like? Would you want to make friends with him? Why? If you were with the others when they voted for a chief, who would you vote for? Why? On a page of your notebook, make two columns. At the top of one, write 'Ralph' and at the top of the other write 'Jack'. Now list, in each column, first the characteristics which you think would make each boy a good chief, and then the characteristics which you think would make each boy a poor chief. Which of the two comes out with the most points in his favour? Is this the boy you chose, earlier?

All the boys who gather together when Ralph blows the conch are wearing different types of school uniform. What sorts of schools do you think they have come from? Do you think these schools are similar to your schools? Or do you think they are very different? Does your school have a uniform? What do you think the point of a uniform is?

What sort of school has a choir? Does your school have one? Jot down in your notebook what sort of special clothes the members of Jack's choir are wearing. Where would you see a choir in these clothes now?

Why do you think the choir members vote for Jack 'with dreary obedience'? (p. 24).

Read pages 33–4 again. Why is Jack unable to kill the piglet? What do you think he feels when he wants to kill it and is unable to? How would you feel? Do you think it makes any difference that he is not alone? What effect does it have on him that the others see him fail to kill the animal?

Apart from Ralph, Piggy and Jack, who are the other boys we meet in the first chapter? Jot down their names. How many boys do you think there are altogether?

After Ralph is chosen as chief, he decides that the first thing they must do is explore the island. Write down on one page of your notebook what you think Jack would have chosen to do first if he had been chief. Is it different from what Ralph chose? If you had been chosen chief, what would you have decided must be done first?

Now that you have thought some more about the first chapter, think about who this story is written for. You will have realized at once that all the characters are boys and you will be fairly sure that no adults are likely to appear during the rest of the story. Do you think, since the story is about boys, that the book is a children's story? Jot down your reasons for your opinion. Sometimes there are stories about adults written for children; and sometimes there are stories about children written for adults. What are some of the ways in which we can tell who a story is mainly written for? Are any of these ways clear in the first chapter of *Lord of the Flies*? After you have written down who you think this story is mainly written for, exchange your notes with someone else. Have you and your partner noticed the same things? Keep your notes so you can add to them later when we think about the themes in this story.

CHAPTER 2, *pp. 35–51*

After Ralph, Jack and Simon return from the first exploration of the island, Ralph blows the conch to call a meeting. What does he tell the others? Piggy points out that not only do they not know themselves where they are, but that no one else knows they are on the island. Why do you think the others are silent when he says that? What would you be thinking if you were part of the group?

Ralph reassures them all that it is a good island and that they will have fun. Some boys remember stories they have read about people being marooned on islands. Read page 38 again and you will see the titles of some of those stories. What are they? Have you read any of them yourself? You could check whether your school or local library has any of these stories or any others about being stuck on an island. When were these stories written? Does it make a difference to you if a story was written a long time ago? Can you still enjoy it? Does reading *Lord of the Flies* make you want to read stories about being on an island which were written before you or your parents were born? Jot down in one paragraph what your reasons are.

During the meeting, a small six-year-old, with a birthmark on his face, is made to tell something to the others.

Read page 39 again and then write down in your own words what he tells them. Do you think he has really seen a 'snake-thing'? What is he afraid of? Read pages 39 to 40 again and then write down in one paragraph how Ralph reassures the little ones that they need not be afraid. Now imagine you are Piggy. Write down another paragraph where you invent what Piggy would have said to reassure them. Is it different from what Ralph says? Why do you think that is so?

Jack agrees with Ralph and says there is no 'beastie'; but he adds that if there were, they would simply kill it. Why do you think Jack is so excited by the thought of killing things? Do you find the thought exciting? Why?

Read page 41 again. Ralph is telling the others that they will be rescued in the end. Everyone claps when he finishes speaking. Piggy admires him and Jack smirks. What is smirking? If you are not sure, check the word in your dictionary. Jot down on half a page of your notebook why you think Piggy and Jack have such different reactions to Ralph's speech.

The meeting breaks up in confusion when Ralph suggests they make a fire to attract attention to themselves, to make it easier for any rescuers to find them. Everyone except Piggy rushes off to build the fire. Why are they all so excited? Why do you think Piggy does not join them?

Write down in one paragraph what you would feel if you were helping to build the fire. Now imagine you are Piggy, standing alone with the conch and watching the others rush off. What does Piggy feel? Write another paragraph, this time setting out what Piggy is thinking and feeling while the others are building the fire. One thing you will have noticed is that when Piggy is exasperated with the others, he often mutters that they are 'just like kids'. What does he mean? What are 'kids' like? Is Piggy different from a 'kid'? In what ways does he strike you as being like the others sometimes, and being very different from the others at other times? You will have realized that although Piggy is a boy like the others, he is somehow rather like a grown-up as well. Do you think this might mean that Piggy likes grown-ups more than the others do? Why do you think so?

When Piggy stays with Ralph, he is showing what some people call loyalty. What is loyalty? Write down on one page of your notebook an incident you remember when someone was loyal to you. Is loyalty something you think people find helpful in their friendships? Or not?

Read page 43 again. The boys are busy finding wood to make the fire. We are told that Ralph and Jack, sitting together on a dead tree limb, share 'that strange invisible light of friendship, adventure and content'. Jot down, on one page, what you think Ralph and Jack like about each other. How does each boy know that the other boy likes him? Have you felt the 'invisible light' we are told about? How do you know when someone is your friend?

Ralph and Jack both feel very silly when they realize they have built a huge pile of wood for a fire without first working out how they are going to light it. No one has any matches. What solution do they come up with? Why does Jack snatch Piggy's glasses, rather than asking him to lend them so that the lens will ignite the fire? Although Piggy protests at Jack's rude treatment of him, no one defends him. Why do you think that is so?

The fire burns immediately, but then dies out. Piggy points out that they could never keep such a huge flame going anyway. This remark irritates Jack enormously. He taunts Piggy and tells him to shut up. Read pages 45–7 again. Why do Piggy and Jack dislike each other so much? In one paragraph, imagine you are Jack and write down what you think of Piggy. Now, in another paragraph, imagine you are Piggy and write down what you think of Jack. Which boy do you find it easier to imagine being? Which boy do you prefer? Why is that?

The next fire the boys kindle rushes quickly out of control. Read page 48 again. What is Piggy's reaction to this huge blaze? Read page 49 again. What is Ralph's reaction? Is it different from Piggy's? What does the writer mean when he says the power of the fire makes Ralph 'savage'? Write down in one paragraph what you think the word 'savage' means. Have you ever been made savage, like Ralph? What do you think causes savage feelings in anyone? Are they enjoyable feelings? Are they frightening? Would you be frightened to see someone made savage?

Only Piggy is not excited by the huge fire. He loses his temper instead. Read page 50 again. Jot down in your own words what Piggy says to the others. What does he think they should have done first? Do you agree? Why is that? Why are the others irritated when Piggy says something reasonable?

Read page 51 again. The boys realize something dreadful may have happened as a result of the huge blaze. What is it?

CHAPTER 3, *pp. 52–62*

In the third chapter we are shown striking differences between three of the main characters in the story: Ralph, Jack and Simon. Read the chapter again and jot down what each of the three boys is mainly interested in doing.

Let us consider Jack first. You will have noticed there is something odd about him; that he is sometimes 'mad'. What kind of madness do you think it is? Contrast Jack's madness with Ralph's reasonableness. Now think about Ralph. You will have seen that Ralph wants their shelters to be finished as soon as possible and that he is exasperated with the littluns, who keep going off to play or swim. You will have noticed, too, that Ralph wants the shelters to be a home, not only to protect them all from the sun and the rain, but also to help them to combat the fears and nightmares many boys suffer from at night. Ralph finds it important that these fears are quelled, because they suggest that where the boys are is not 'a good island'. What do you think this means? What does Ralph feel can make the island good or bad?

Jack does not understand Ralph's insistence on building the shelters. He has his own obsession. He needs to kill a pig. Read pages 55–60 again. Now write down the argument between Ralph and Jack in your own words. You should take about one page of your notebook. Why are the two boys so angry with one another? Can two people who are friends be as angry as Ralph and Jack are? Which boy can you understand better? Do you think finished shelters are more important than fresh meat? Or that fresh meat is the most important priority? Or do you think both boys are wrong? Would you put something quite different first?

You will have noticed that none of the other boys share either Ralph's obsession, or Jack's. Jack's choir members are willing to help him hunt, but when he says they may go, they prefer to rush off and play rather than stay and hunt some more. Only Simon stays to help Ralph with the shelters. What do you think makes Ralph and Jack more obsessed than the others? Is it something to do with being leaders? What do you think makes someone a leader? Are you a leader or a follower? How do you know? Jot down a list of five characteristics which you would expect to find in a leader. Now add five characteristics which you might also find, but which you would dislike. Which of the characteristics you have noted does Ralph have? Which does Jack have? Compare your list with someone else's who is reading *Lord of the Flies*. Are the two lists very similar, or very different? Would you feel safer with Ralph as chief? Or with Jack?

Ralph tells Jack that Simon is the only one who helps him. Imagine for a moment that you are Simon. What makes Simon want to help Ralph? Is there something he would rather be doing instead? Why does Simon help Ralph rather than Jack?

Write down on one page of your notebook what you think makes Simon creep away into the jungle by himself. Ralph and Jack think Simon has joined the others in the bathing-pool. None of the others would realize that Simon wants to be by himself. What makes Simon different in this way? Do you ever want to leave a group and go off by yourself? What does it feel like to leave the group? What is different about being alone from being in the group?

Simon finds a natural shelter and creeps into it. What does he notice? Is he afraid? Or not? Why do you think that is so? Are you afraid when you are alone? Why is that? Write down in your own words on half a page what you think Simon is feeling as he watches and listens in his hiding-place.

CHAPTER 4, *pp. 63–82*

Read page 63 again. The writer tells us that the boys have become used to a rhythm in the passing of the day. Jot down the stages of this rhythm. Now write down, in your own words, how the sun makes everything on the island look different, depending on what time of day it is.

The day's rhythm makes hope unnecessary. Which hope does the writer mean? Think about a time when you were so happy that you forgot what you were supposed to be doing. Jot down five words which help to describe this sort of happiness. Now write a paragraph in your own words describing what it is like at midday on the island. You will need to notice both what you can see and how you feel.

We are told next that 'the northern European tradition of work, play and food' makes it impossible for the boys to adapt completely to this rhythm. Jot down what you imagine they would do if they could adapt completely. Remember to say when they would work, play and eat. What do you think the 'northern European tradition' is? Perhaps you have heard of a different tradition, one characteristic of a part of Africa, for example, or South America, or southern Europe. Jot down some of the differences in a tradition which is followed in some part of the world other than northern Europe. Now think about how we live in Britain. Does the climate control our lives more than we are aware of? Why do we do our sleeping at night, for instance? Jot down five ways in which what we do is regulated by our climate.

Now read pages 64–5 again and then write a short list which shows the differences between the way the 'biguns' live and the way the 'littluns' live. Why does the writer want us to notice these differences? Might it help to explain why some are more easily led than others? Think for a moment about the littluns. Why do they have diarrhoea all the time? What are some of the games they like playing? Imagine how your life would be if you could do what you wanted all day long, day after day. Would you like your new life better than the one you have now? Or not? Why is that?

Roger, one of the biguns, follows a younger boy called Henry and starts to throw stones at him. You will have noticed that Roger does not dare to aim straight in order to hit Henry directly. What stops him? The writer says he is stopped by 'the taboo of the old life' which protects Henry like a shield. The taboo includes parents and school and policemen and the law. Write down in your own words how you think this taboo works. Do you agree that it can work like this? What stops you, for instance, from attacking someone you know? On the island, there are no parents, schools or policemen. Do you think the writer means that whether real parents, teachers or policemen are actually present or not, we somehow learn to carry their views and their voices around inside us? Why do you think some of us feel the taboo against harming people more strongly than others seem to? Can you imagine Piggy, for example, wanting to throw stones at Henry? Do you think you would want to? Or not? Why is that?

Next, Jack explains to Roger that he thinks the reason for his hunting failures is that the pigs can see him too easily. Do you agree? Jack says he has found some coloured clay and he wants to camouflage himself with it. When he has painted himself and is peering at his reflection in a pool, he sees staring back at him 'an awesome stranger'. Think for a moment about the possibility that it is not so much the pigs Jack has to deceive in order to be able to kill them, as himself. He needs to think he is someone different from how he has been before. In order to kill pigs he needs, perhaps, to get rid of those same taboos of civilization which have just prevented Roger from attacking Henry with stones. The 'awesome stranger' who looks back at Jack is a different version of himself, capable of 'bloodthirsty snarling'. Write down on one page what you think Jack is feeling and imagining as he dances and snarls.

Meanwhile Ralph, Piggy, Simon and Maurice see a ship passing along the horizon. Ralph, in a panic, realizes that their smoke signal may not be visible. He rushes, followed by the others, to the fire. Indeed, the fire has gone out. Jack and his hunters, who promised to keep it alight, have failed to do so. Ralph's rage is unbounded. Can you understand the panic and the rage Ralph feels? Jot down five words which will help you remember why he is so angry. 'Frustration' might be one word, for example.

The four boys see a procession coming towards them and realize gradually that it is Jack and his hunters carrying a dead pig and chanting as they walk. Read pages 75–7 again. Now write down in your own words the argument between Jack and Ralph. You will have noticed that for Jack, the spilling of blood and the sense of power it releases in him, are of the most urgent importance; whereas for Ralph, the constant flame of the fire is most urgent. The writer makes us understand the importance of both. But do the boys understand each other? Why is that?

Jack will tolerate Ralph's rage, but not Piggy's criticism. When Piggy ticks him off, he punches Piggy and causes his glasses to break. Write down in one paragraph why you think Jack does not hit Ralph as he has attacked Piggy. When Jack apologizes for letting the fire go out and begins to build it again, Ralph asserts his chieftainship by simply remaining silent. Why do you think remaining silent is more effective than arguing or commanding? Read page 79 again. Now jot down why you think the link between Jack and Ralph has been broken and why a link between Ralph and Piggy has been established. Notice how Ralph treats Piggy with a new respect. Why do you think Ralph's feelings about Piggy have changed?

The boys finally become friendly again as they sit around the new fire, roasting and eating the pig-meat. Jack and the other hunters first tell the story of how they killed the pig and then they re-enact it, with Maurice pretending to be the pig. Why is Ralph 'envious and resentful' as he watches them? Why does he say he will call a meeting? In your dictionary, find the meaning of the word 'ritual'. Now jot down what you think makes Jack and the others develop the ritual of re-enacting the hunt and the kill. Do you think Jack hunts only to have meat to eat? Or for another reason as well? What other reason can you think of? If you were with the boys, whose feelings would you understand better: Ralph's or Jack's? Now jot down what you think Simon feels; and what you think Piggy feels.

CHAPTER 5, *pp. 83–103*

As Ralph walks alone, preparing himself for the meeting he has called, he becomes aware of new discoveries about himself and about life. Read pages 83–5 again and then list what you think these discoveries are. You will have noticed that he is provoked to these new thoughts partly because he feels uncomfortable in his frayed and filthy clothing.

The meeting begins with Ralph explaining that he has not called it to 'have fun' but to 'put things straight'. What do you think he means? What is the difference between these two things? One difference Ralph points to is that they enjoy deciding things in their meetings but that then the decisions are not carried out. Read pages 86–8 again. Now make a list of the rules the boys have already made, but not kept.

Ralph's next point is that they must decide how to deal with the fear they all feel. He says they must deal with it by talking about it. Write down on one page your own opinion about whether talking about things – fear, in this case – helps us to understand and cope better. You will notice that several boys take the conch and express an opinion. Jot down the names of the boys who speak. Now jot down the main point each one makes. You can see that Jack's view, for example, is that fear is something people must endure; but a 'beast' cannot have caused it, he argues, because he's explored the whole island and hasn't seen one. Piggy agrees that there's no beast, adding that life is 'scientific'. What does he mean? Jot down in your own words how life might be 'scientific'. Piggy goes on to say that the only real fear is being frightened of other people. Do you agree with him? Phil, a littlun, says he has *seen* a beast; but it turns out to have been Simon out alone at night. Percival, another littlun, says the beast comes out of the sea.

Why does Ralph find all this talk insane? Think about walking with a crowd of people in the dark. Imagine someone begins to talk about ghosts and monsters. If everyone joins in and takes the talk seriously, what do you think begins to happen? Why does everything seem different in the dark? Some children are afraid of the dark. Jot down briefly what you think it is about the dark which brings out fear and makes people more ready to fear ghosts and monsters than they are in the daylight.

Now consider what Simon says. Do you agree that fear is 'only us'? Jot down what you think this means.

Like Ralph, Piggy finds all the talking about beasts and ghosts absurd and worrying. He asks the others whether they are humans, or animals or savages. He asks what the grown-ups will think. Jot down what you think the differences are between humans, animals and savages. To which of the three does Piggy think they belong? Do you agree? What do you think grown-ups would think of them killing pigs, letting the fire go out and talking about 'beasts'? What do you think of them? Is what you think different from what grown-ups would think? Why is that?

Imagine you are an adult who has just found the boys and who has listened in on the meeting without the boys knowing. Now write on one page what you would say to the meeting when you stepped out to show yourself to the boys. Are you cross? Are you admiring? Are you sorry for them? What do you tell them to do next?

Jack and Ralph argue, again because Jack has attacked Piggy. Ralph tries to take control by reminding Jack that he, Ralph, has been chosen chief. Jack challenges him, asking why choosing should make any difference. Do you think choosing makes any difference? Jot down why you think so.

Read pages 100–103 again. What are Ralph and Piggy discussing? Write a list showing the reasons Ralph gives for thinking he should give up being chief. Now write a list showing Piggy's reasons for persuading him to remain chief. Which reasons do you find most convincing? Do you think Ralph should give up being chief? Why do you think so? Both boys, together with Simon, think grown-ups would be behaving differently. Do you agree? What might grown-ups do differently?

CHAPTER 6, *pp. 104–19*

Ralph, Piggy and Simon had wanted a sign from grown-ups and, while they sleep, one comes. Read pages 104–5 again. Now write down in your own words what the sign is. Notice that the figure falling from the skies comes from a battle so high up that none of its noise can be heard. What kind of a sign is the dead parachutist? Of what is he a sign? Is the world of grown-ups really in the better state that Ralph and Piggy have assumed? If the boys were awake and could see the body dropping, what message might it bring them? What would they think of grown-ups? Are grown-ups really so different from themselves?

The twins, Sam and Eric, are on fire duty but have been sleeping and the fire is nearly out. As they build it up, the new flames light up the mountain-top. What do the twins see in the flickering light? Write a short paragraph describing first what the twins actually see and then what they think they see. There are many different ways of perceiving things. What do you think makes someone see shapes and shadows that are not really there?

Sam and Eric rush in terror to tell Ralph what they have seen. Ralph calls a meeting. Read pages 109–10 again and then write a list of all the characteristics the twins say that the 'beast' they have seen possessed. Which of these characteristics could they have actually seen? Which ones have they invented?

What does the meeting resolve to do? You will have noticed that there is some confusion about whether hunting the 'beast' or restarting the fire is the more urgent priority. Despite Jack's efforts to humiliate him, Piggy is left to mind the littluns. Why do you think no one realizes that Piggy's glasses will be necessary to restart the fire? Might it be that even Ralph is more concerned now to find the 'beast'?

As they make their way, Simon thinks about what they have been told and finds he still cannot really believe in the 'beast'. When he tries to picture what Sam and Eric have described, all he can imagine is 'the picture of a human at once heroic and sick'. Write down in one paragraph why you think Simon is not as convinced as are the others. What do you think makes some boys, more than others, believe in the 'beast'?

Read pages 115–19 again. Now write down in your own words the conversation between Ralph and Jack. What excites Jack? What is Ralph most interested in? What do they disagree about? Is there anything they agree about? Now add a paragraph explaining what the other boys want to do. Why do you think they are so easily distracted? Why do you think Ralph is the only one to be 'nuts on the signal' of the fire?

We are now half way through the story. It will be helpful to try to bring together all the things you will have noticed and written about so far. To make this task easier, take a fresh section of your notebook and on separate pages make the following headings:

(1) Main events
(2) Main characters
(3) Main ideas
(4) Main judgements

(1) MAIN EVENTS

Begin this page as a letter. Imagine you have been an extra boy on the island: *not* Ralph or Piggy or Jack or Simon or any of the others, but someone who is not in the story. Just be yourself. Write your letter to someone you know will be interested in what you have observed; it may be a friend or a teacher or a member of your family or even someone you do not know very well. In your letter, explain all the important things that have happened so far. Make sure you record the main events in the order in which they have happened. You may take extra pages if you wish.

(2) MAIN CHARACTERS

On this page, set out what each main character is like. Make sure you include what he looks like, what he is interested in and what the others think of him. When you have done that, add what you think of him. You may take extra pages if you wish.

(3) MAIN IDEAS

Here you will set out *what* you think the writer wants to point out. The best way to do this is to explain *how* he tells the story. Does he, for example, tell you all the facts one after another? Or does he do something different? One way to tackle this question is to take two or three passages and look at them very closely. One might be, for instance, the passage describing the falling parachutist. Are the words only giving information? Or do they give, as well, indications of insight and knowledge into some aspects of human nature? Which words or phrases do this?

You will find it helpful, too, to note the symbols and images which are repeated. Some important images, for example, are the fire and the hunt. However, the writer does not tell us things like 'the fire represents being reasonable' or 'the fire represents wanting to be rescued'. How, then, does the writer make clear to us that the fire, the hunt, the conch, the island itself, all mean more than their physical appearances?

Consider, as well, some of the arguments the boys have. How can you tell what view the writer himself takes about some of the points discussed? You may take as many pages as you wish to make your notes about the book's main ideas.

(4) MAIN JUDGEMENTS

On this page, imagine you are writing a diary. This means you are writing to yourself. Tell yourself what you think about this story so far. Note whether it is a good story or a poor one and why you think so. Note, too, which characters you like and dislike and why you do. Note whether you agree or not with the points the writer is making. Especially make sure you note what you think about the different reactions the boys have to the 'beast'. You may take more pages if you wish.

CHAPTER 7, *pp. 120–36*

While the boys are still on the move to find the 'beast' and restart the fire, the sun rises to its zenith and the midday heat becomes overwhelmingly oppressive. Ralph sends a message to Jack for the group to rest and eat. Read pages 120–21 again. You will see that Ralph is self-conscious about his appearance. He feels extremely uncomfortable. When he looks at the others, he realizes that they, too, have succumbed to a lower standard. What do you think Ralph means by a 'standard'? Jot down why you think Ralph is suddenly bothered by matted hair and ragged clothes.

Think for a moment about what differences clothes make. Remember how Jack wanted to paint his skin in order to be able to kill the pigs. Do you think we wear clothes only for practical reasons, such as protection from the climate? Can you think of any other reasons?

Read the first half of page 122 again. Here Ralph stares at the sea. What does he see? What does he feel? What do you think the 'brute obtuseness' of the ocean is? The island is, of course, cut off from the rest of the world by ocean. Jot down in one paragraph what you think the ocean means to Ralph as he sits and looks at it. Remember to include why you think it makes him feel 'condemned'.

Simon interrupts Ralph to reassure him, saying, 'You'll get back to where you came from.' How do you think Simon knows that Ralph is feeling hopeless about ever being rescued? Ralph wonders why Simon is so sure, but Simon simply repeats his conviction. Ralph tells him he is 'batty', which Simon vigorously denies. Do you think Simon is 'batty'? What makes Ralph think so? What makes a person 'batty'?

When the boys set off again they find fresh pig-droppings. This find encourages Jack to persuade Ralph and the others that as well as hunting the 'beast', they can also hunt for fresh meat. Ralph begins to day-dream. Why do you think his day-dreaming begins at this point? Read pages 123–4 again. Now write down in your own words the part of his childhood that Ralph thinks of. Remember what you have noticed about Ralph's awareness of losing 'standards'. Might this day-dream be part of this awareness? Might it be part of his realization that 'normal' life is immensely different from this new life? What do you think the main differences are? Jot down five that come immediately to mind.

Next Ralph wounds a charging boar. He feels very proud. The others are admiring and excited. Soon they begin to re-enact the experience, with Robert pretending to be the wild pig. Can you remember who played the pig last time they performed this ritual?

Read page 126 again. Now write a paragraph in your own words describing what you think happens as the ritual develops. Why is Robert so afraid? Why does Ralph find the desire to hunt 'over-mastering'?

What time of day is it when they set off again? Who offers to go alone through the jungle to tell Piggy and the littluns that the hunters will not be back yet? Read pages 127–31 again. There is an argument between Jack and Ralph. Jot down what they argue about. What does Ralph realize about Jack's attitude towards him?

The boys struggle to the top of the mountain in search of the 'beast', goaded by Jack's mockery. Jack, Ralph and Roger creep forward towards the top. Read pages 135–6 again. Write down in one paragraph what the three boys see. Why do you think they see a 'beast' instead of a dead parachutist? What is so fearful to them? Imagine you are there with them. Are you as frightened? Does it make a difference that it is night-time? Why do you think people are afraid of dead bodies? When you have thought about these questions, write down what you think about this kind of fear. Remember to consider what you think about Simon's opinion, that the 'beast' must be inside themselves. Remember, as well, that Piggy said the only thing to be really afraid of is other people. A dead man in a parachute cannot possibly do any actual harm to the boys. Nevertheless, we can understand their fear. What helps us to understand it?

Remember a time when you were as afraid as the three boys are. Now write down what you remember as if you were writing a report for a newspaper. You need to make clear exactly where you were, who else was there, what the place was like, what time of day it was and what had led up to your being there. As you write, try to describe very accurately what you saw and heard, so that it will be clear to the reader what things were really like and how you felt about them.

Now jot down which you think is more frightening: a real beast or monster, or one which may come to you in a nightmare or which you might be told about by someone else? Large numbers of people, for example, very much like watching horror films. They often seem to enjoy the experience of being frightened. Why do you think that is so? Do you enjoy being frightened in that way? Why is that? Do children enjoy this sort of fear more than adults? Or the other way around? Do men enjoy it more than women, boys than girls? Or the other way around? Why might there be these differences?

CHAPTER 8, *pp. 137–59*

Ralph tells Piggy he has seen the 'beast'. Piggy finds this very hard to believe, despite his trust in Ralph. Nevertheless, his reaction is very practical. He asks what they are going to do.

Imagine you are Simon. Now jot down what you hope the others are going to do. Imagine, next, that you are Piggy. Jot down what you think the others ought to do. Lastly, imagine you are Ralph. Jot down what you think you ought to tell the others to do.

Jack calls a meeting. Read pages 139–41 again. Now jot down what takes place during this meeting. Why does Jack ask the others to vote against continuing to have Ralph as chief? Why do you think the others go on supporting Ralph, in spite of Jack's challenge? What is Jack's real reason for deciding to leave the group?

Simon suggests they should go back and climb the mountain, but everyone laughs at him. Why do you think no one takes Simon seriously? Does the writer take Simon seriously? What makes you think so?

Who suggests making a new fire down on the beach? The others are enthusiastic and help readily, to start with. But the new fire dies down and Ralph and Piggy realize that many of the others have drifted off. Where have they gone? Why do you think they have left Ralph, Piggy, Sam and Eric? Do you think you would have left, too? Or would you have stayed? Why is that?

Read pages 147–51 again. Jack is near the end of the island with the boys who have joined him. You will have noticed that even though the meeting supported Ralph, most of the boys subsequently joined Jack. Does this mean meetings are only 'talk'? Think about groups or clubs you may have belonged to. Have you ever noticed a similar situation, where a meeting decided something which the group later forgot or did not do? What is it that people agree to in a meeting?

Imagine you are planning an outing. You hold a meeting of everyone who is going on the outing and in the meeting they all agree to a timetable and rules that you suggest. But during the outing, everyone seems to forget what was agreed in the meeting and the outing is a disaster. Write about a page describing the meeting and the subsequent outing and remember to include your own feelings about the result.

Jack, like Ralph, has a sort of meeting with the others, but there are differences. One important difference is that there is no conch. Jot down what difference you think that makes. Now add, in your own words, what Jack tells the others they are going to do. Why do you think the others find it easier to do what Jack commands than what Ralph has asked?

The hunt is successful. The boys corner a sow suckling her piglets and they kill her. Write about a page which shows what you think and how you feel when Roger and Jack spill the sow's blood. Now jot down what the boys do with the carcass of the dead pig.

Having killed their fresh meat, Jack and his followers suddenly realize a difficulty they had not thought of earlier. Yes, you will remember it is the problem of starting a fire to cook the meat. How can they solve this problem? Jot down the solution Jack offers.

Lastly, Jack does something he has not done before. He offers a gift to the 'beast'. What is the gift? Why does he offer it? Why does he think this might placate the 'beast'? Or do you think he does not really believe that it will? Does he offer the gift to impress the others? Are they impressed? Why do you think so? Do you think offering the gift helps the others to feel less frightened? Why is that?

While Ralph and Piggy stay by the fire on the beach and Jack and his followers kill the sow, Simon has crept away into the jungle to be alone. Read pages 151–2 again. It is clear that Simon's hiding-place is near the spot where Jack stakes the sow's head. What thoughts and feelings does Simon have as he stares at the dead head? Jot down in your own words what you think the writer means by having Simon see in the pig's face 'the infinite cynicism of adult life'. Why is Simon sure that everything is 'a bad business'? Simon names the head to himself as the 'Lord of the Flies'. What do you think he means by using this phrase? What do the flies do? What are they gorged with? Note what you think about this passage so you can remember it later when we consider the book's themes.

Down on the beach, Ralph and Piggy are talking things over. Ralph asks Piggy 'what makes things break up like they do?' Jot down what your own answer would be to this question.

After Jack, Maurice and Robert, painted like savages, have raided Ralph's fire, those on the beach prepare for a meeting. Ralph admits he would like to have fun and be a savage, too, but that they must put the fire first. But eating some of Jack's fresh meat is more attractive at that moment to the others.

Imagine you are there with them. Now jot down how you argue with yourself about the conflict between wanting to have fun and eat meat and the need to keep the fire going. How do you decide which to do? Which is easier? Why is keeping the fire going not 'fun'? What makes something 'fun'?

Now read pages 158–9 again. Simon is imagining a conversation with the 'Lord of the Flies'. He feels 'one of his times' coming on. What do you think these 'times' are? Might Simon suffer from something like epilepsy? Look up the word epilepsy in your dictionary. Sometimes people with conditions like epilepsy experience trances or fits or visions in which they see or think or feel unusual things, or things the rest of us may not be aware of. The writer does not mean us to think the pig's head actually speaks to Simon. What is important is that it seems so to the boy, because the dialogue he feels he is having with the head provides a way for him to understand how things are. Write down on one page in your own words what you think Simon learns during his trance or vision.

Have you ever had an experience like Simon's? Or heard someone else tell such an experience? What do you think a person like Jack would make of it, if you told him about it? Why do you think so? Are people like Simon laughed at a lot by others? Why do you think that is? Laughing is often a way of denying something. Do you think the other boys would want to deny Simon's experience if he told them about it? Why do you think so?

CHAPTER 9, *pp. 160–70*

Notice that the opening paragraph of this chapter describes an impending storm. Read the paragraph carefully and note down all the words which suggest heat. You will find, for example, the phrase 'heated air' and the fact that the air from the sea is 'hot'. But you will have noted, too, words like 'brassy' and 'brooded' because they *feel* hot. Now jot down the *effect* of these words on your sense of what the coming storm might be like. How might this storm, for instance, differ from the storms you are used to? Think for a moment, as well, about whether this storm might *represent* something human in the story, at the same time as being part of the natural conditions of the island. When you have considered this suggestion, jot down the conclusions you have come to and your reasons for thinking so.

Simon, his fit having passed, is sleeping in his hide-out. When he wakes, tired and numbed, he begins walking and sees something flap in the wind. Next he sees a 'humped thing' sit up and look down at him. Yes, it is the dead parachutist's body. Unlike the others who came this way earlier, Simon does not flee in fear from the sight, but hides his face and toils on. Why do you think he has this different reaction? Why is he not afraid in the way they were? Jot down your reasons for thinking so.

Simon goes right up to the body and explores it. Note down what he sees. You will be surprised, perhaps, by his ability to give close attention to the details of what he sees. Jot down what you think makes him able to observe something so unknown to him and so potentially frightening, without being forced into a panic.

Next Simon loosens the tangled parachute cords so that the body is rescued from 'the wind's indignity'. Note down what you think this phrase means.

As he looks along the beach, Simon concludes that the others have moved camp. He realizes that he must tell them what the 'beast' really is and to assure them that it is harmless.

Read pages 162–3 again. Ralph and Piggy are alone near the pool. How do they react to the approaching storm? What makes them decide to join Jack's party? Do you think it has anything to do with the coming storm? What makes you think so? Jot down your reasons.

Read page 164 again. Now write two paragraphs in your own words: in the first, imagine you are Jack, with your meat roasting and your tribe having fun around you; and describe what you feel like when Ralph and Piggy arrive. In your second paragraph, imagine you are Piggy and describe how you feel as you approach the others with Ralph. You will notice, as you read and write, that the group is once again united by laughing at Piggy. Why do you think that is the one sure thing that so easily can unite all the others? Jot down why you think so.

As the boys finish feasting, Ralph notices that night has fallen 'not with a calm beauty but with the threat of violence'. What do you think these words mean? Jot down how you think the writer has made you believe them.

Now read pages 165–6 again. As the storm breaks, Jack once again challenges Ralph for leadership of the whole group. How does Ralph resist? Piggy wants Ralph to come away, saying 'there's going to be trouble'. What kind of trouble do you think he means? Do you agree with Piggy's premonition? What makes you think so? Has the sensing of trouble got anything to do with the impending storm?

Jack orders the others to begin their ritual dance. At the height of their frenzy and chanting, with lightning and thunder breaking over them, 'a thing' crawls out of the forest into the circle. What is the 'thing'? Yes, it is Simon. Why does he come 'darkly' and 'uncertainly'? He tries to tell the others about the dead parachutist. Why do you think they cannot hear him? What do they do instead?

Read carefully the bottom half of page 168 and the top of page 169. Which two important events happen? Now write on one page how

Simon is killed. Include *why* you think he dies in this way. Could he have avoided his death? Why do you think so? Do you understand the frenzy that drives the others? What helps you to understand it? Are you sad that Simon dies? Or angry? Why is that? What else do you feel about his death? Jot down your reasons for feeling like this.

What happens to the body of the dead parachutist? What causes this? Will the disappearance of the 'beast' make a difference to the others? Why do you think so?

Jot down what things are like on the island after the storm. Which words used by the writer do you find specially striking? Notice how now, instead of 'hot' words, the writer uses 'cool' ones. Note down what these are. Which 'beast' lies huddled on the beach (p. 169)? What finally happens to Simon's body? What causes this?

CHAPTER 10, *pp. 171–86*

Read pages 171–4 again. What are Ralph and Piggy discussing? Jot down what Ralph's views are and then what Piggy's are. Whose views do you think are the more accurate? Do you agree with Ralph that Simon was murdered? Or with Piggy, that it was an accident? Why is that? Ralph says Piggy was outside the circle and asks him 'Didn't you see what we – what they did?' Why do you think Ralph first says 'we' and then 'they'? Do you think Ralph helped to kill Simon? Or not? What difference does it make to your view of Ralph when you think about whether he did or did not take part in the killing?

Piggy says Simon was 'batty' and that he should not have crawled in out of the dark. Do you agree? Why do you think so? Did Simon 'ask for it'?

Think for a few moments about victims of violence generally: women who are raped, people who are beaten and killed. Do you think some people 'ask for it'? What does this mean? Does it make a difference to how you feel about their pain and suffering? Write, on two pages, two stories: in the first, write about a victim who 'asks for it'; and in the second, write about a victim who *doesn't* 'ask for it'. Now compare your two stories.

Do you think there is really any difference between the victims? Is it possible, do you think, that no one 'asks for it' but that we – like Piggy – find it easier to face the horror of victimization if we decide that the victim was somehow partly to blame for what happens? Think again about Simon. Do you think the writer's attitude is that Simon 'asks for it'? What makes you think so?

Read pages 174–5 again. Why do you think Ralph and Piggy agree with each other that they were both 'on the outside'? Do you think they were? How does it make them feel better to tell this to each other? When Sam and Eric arrive, what do the four boys tell each other? What is the 'unspoken knowledge' in the air?

Roger goes to join the tribe and finds Jack busy holding court as chief. Jot down what Jack has done so far as chief and what he plans to do. Read page 177 again. Why do you think Jack tells the others that the beast cannot be killed? What does he mean? Remember that Simon had thought the same thing. What were Simon's reasons? Are Jack's the same or not? Notice that when Jack says the beast cannot be killed, the others all understand that there must be more killing. Jot down how the writer makes that clear.

Read page 178 again. Why does Jack blush? How will the tribe be able to start another fire? Ralph and Piggy try to keep their fire on the beach alight. How many others are with them? Are there enough boys to maintain the fire? What do you think will happen to these few if they cannot keep the fire going?

Read page 184 again. What happens while Ralph, Piggy, Sam and Eric lie in their shelter trying to sleep? During the fighting, Ralph and Eric make a mistake. What is it? Who has Ralph been fighting? What happens to Piggy during the fighting?

What was the reason for the attack on Ralph and the other three? Do you think it was as straightforward as simply wanting to be able to make fire independently from Ralph and Piggy? Is it possible that Jack also wanted an excuse for a fight, so that he could win against Ralph?

At the end of the chapter, Jack feels he is 'chief now in truth'. Why does he think so? Do you agree? Why is that? What do you think is Jack's opinion now of the conch? Do you think Ralph is still chief? What makes you think so? What would make Jack chief? What would make Ralph chief? Which system of finding the chief would you support more? Why is that? Jot down your reasons for thinking so.

CHAPTER 11, *pp. 187–201*

Piggy asks Ralph to call a meeting, even though there are only four of them together now. Ralph agrees. Why do you think Piggy wants a meeting, called by the conch, rather than an ordinary talk between them? Jot down your reasons for thinking so.

Ralph is angry and puzzled about the others stealing Piggy's glasses and he is seriously worried about their now not being able to keep the fire going. He says the others could have had fire if they had asked. Do you agree that Ralph would have given Jack fire if Jack had simply asked? Why do you think so? Why do you think Jack needed to steal it?

Piggy wants his glasses back and wants Ralph to decide something. Ralph thinks about going to the tribe and suggests that they smarten up first, because they are not savages really. Do you agree that they are not savages? What difference do you think smartening up would make? Why do you think so?

Read page 189 again. It is Piggy, not Ralph, who makes a decision. What is his decision? Look at the paragraph beginning, 'I'm going to him with this conch in my hands.' It is unlike Piggy to speak out quite like this. What do you think gives him the confidence to do so?

After you have read the whole paragraph carefully, write down in your own words what Piggy says. Why do you think he wants to take the conch with him? What does he mean when he says he will not ask Jack to be a 'sport', but to do what is right? What does 'right' mean here? Do you think Piggy's speech is brave? What makes you think so? Jot down your reasons.

Ralph, Sam and Eric, although they feel afraid of Jack, agree to go with Piggy. Ralph hands Piggy the conch and Piggy flushes with pride. Why do you think he is so proud?

Read pages 192–3. The four boys set off, with the conch, towards Castle Rock, where the tribe must be. Jot down what you think each boy must be feeling: Ralph, in the lead, followed by Piggy, who can hardly see at all, with Sam and Eric, who are afraid of being unpainted, in the rear. Now imagine you are with them and jot down a paragraph about what you anticipate will happen when you reach the tribe.

When the four reach the neck of land leading to the high rocks, Roger calls 'Halt! Who goes there?' What is Ralph's reply? Do you agree with Ralph that Roger is being 'silly'? Why do you think so?

Read page 194. Ralph says he is calling an assembly but the 'savages' do not respond. Roger throws a stone between Sam and Eric and feels 'a source of power' pulse in him. What do you think this power is? Do you think you have ever felt as Roger does at this moment? If you have, what were the circumstances? If you think you have not, imagine what might cause you to feel like this. Do you think we all have the capacity to enjoy making someone else afraid of us? Or do you think only some of us like that feeling? Why do you think so? Jot down your reasons.

Now write a paragraph describing Jack's arrival. Notice what he looks like. What does he say to Ralph? Jack refuses Ralph's request for Piggy's glasses and challenges Ralph instead. Ralph loses his temper and calls Jack a thief. Why does this make Piggy scream and plead with Ralph to remember him? Do you think Piggy's instinct is right? Does Ralph's losing his temper somehow put Piggy at risk? Jot down why you think so.

Read pages 196–8. After Ralph and Jack fight, Ralph again addresses the others. What are the two points he makes? Why do you think the others are unmoved and take no notice? Is it perhaps because they do not any longer want to be rescued?

Why do you think Jack orders the others to capture Sam and Eric? We are told Jack is 'inspired'. What do you think this means? When Ralph and Jack fight again, each boy knows that it is crucial to win. Why is that so? How does the writer make us aware of it? What will be the result for the winner? What will the result be for the loser?

Read page 199 again. Now write down in your own words what Piggy says to the others. What particular point does he make that causes the others to start clamouring? What do you think makes Roger start to throw stones down towards the four boys? Remember how Roger threw a stone earlier and that it gave him a sense of power.

Now read page 200 again. Roger has 'a sense of delirious abandonment'. What do you think this means? What do you think Roger feels? Write down in your own words how Piggy is killed. Now jot down whether you feel sad or angry or another feeling when you think about his death. Compare what you have written with what you wrote about Simon's death. What are the similarities? What are the differences? Do you think Piggy's death could have been avoided? Why do you think so? Do you think any particular special factors contributed to his death? List what you think these might be.

Jack and the others attack Ralph, but he escapes. Jack and Roger force Sam and Eric to join the tribe. What is the 'nameless authority' Roger wields now? Is it perhaps a special distinction earned by his having killed someone single-handed? The disappearance of the littlun with a birthmark on his face, which happened as a result of the first fire; and the killing of Simon, were not the result of a single hand. Piggy's death, on the other hand, has been directly caused by Roger. Do you think, nevertheless, that the presence of the others has made an important difference? Remember how Roger alone, earlier in the story, threw stones at a younger boy without daring to aim directly at him, because a taboo of civilization somehow prevented him. Do you think the taboo was strong because he was alone? Or do you think the changes that the group of boys have gone through since then have lifted the taboo? Jot down your thoughts about what makes Roger able to kill Piggy.

Imagine you are Roger. Write a paragraph describing how Roger feels now that the others regard him as having a special authority. Are these feelings you would like to have? Or not? Jot down your reasons.

It is clear that despite Roger's new distinction, there seems to be no question that he will challenge Jack for leadership of the tribe. Why do you think that is? What is Jack's leadership based on? Why is Ralph more a threat to him that Roger can ever be?

CHAPTER 12, *pp. 202–23*

Read pages 202–3. Ralph is now alone and in hiding. He realizes that the others will never leave him in peace 'because of that indefinable connection between himself and Jack'. What do you think that indefinable connection is? Remember how, at the beginning, Ralph and Jack sat happily together on a tree-trunk, experiencing the glow of friendship. Has this something to do with the connection that is now so threatening to Ralph? Think for a moment about how love and hatred seem to be closely related to each other. Have you ever experienced a friendship that soured and became bitter? What might cause that to happen? Do you think bitter feelings towards someone who was once a friend can go deeper than they do towards someone you never liked particularly in the first place? Why do you think so? Think now about what has happened between Ralph and Jack. Do you think Ralph has good reason to fear Jack and to deduce that Jack will never stop pursuing him? Why do you think so?

Read page 204 again. Ralph comes across the staked pig's head, now stripped of its flesh, as Simon had encountered it before him. Jot down what goes through Ralph's mind as he stares at the 'Lord of the Flies'. Why does he smash the skull? Does he perhaps feel that the savagery of the others might in some way be lessened or destroyed if this symbol of savagery is smashed? Read again the notes you made about Simon's conversation with the pig's head. Now compare Simon's experience with Ralph's. What are the similarities? What are the differences? Why do you think so?

Read pages 206–9. Ralph appeals to Sam and Eric for friendship. Imagine you are Ralph. Now write on one page all the feelings that pass through you as you peer over the ledge where the twins stand guard. Remember to begin with the fear and isolation Ralph must endure now that he is alone. And remember to go through the reactions Ralph has as he realizes that Sam and Eric now belong to Jack's tribe. Lastly, remember to say how Ralph must feel when he is told to forget 'what's sense' from now on.

Now imagine you are Sam or Eric. Write on one page your feelings when Ralph suddenly appears and asks for your help. Remember the fear of Roger and the others and remember how weak Sam and Eric feel and what makes them afraid.

Sam and Eric tell Ralph that the tribe is preparing to hunt him down during the next day, though they 'don't know' why. What do you think the reason is? What do you think Ralph thinks the reason is?

Read page 210. The twins tell Ralph that Roger has 'sharpened a stick at both ends'. What does this mean? What has been the purpose of such a stick so far? What does the knowledge mean to Ralph? What are Jack and Roger planning to do to him?

After spending a safe night, Ralph wakes to noises heralding the beginning of the hunt. He feels secure in his hiding-place, since he has trusted Sam and Eric to protect him. Then he overhears that Sam and Eric have been frightened and tormented into telling Jack and Roger where he is. Jot down how you think Ralph feels now.

Read pages 213–14. What is the first way in which the tribe tries to kill Ralph? When the huge boulders do not kill him, what does he face next? Read pages 216–17. Jot down what alternatives Ralph has. Now jot down which one he chooses. What is the final method Jack and the tribe use to trap Ralph?

Read page 220. Now imagine you are Ralph. Write on one page what you feel and think and notice as you run for your life. Remember you are running both from the savages and from the fire.

Read page 221. Who does Ralph run into on the beach? Notice that the naval officers explain to Ralph that they were drawn by the smoke rising up from the island. Read pages 222–3. The officer in charge asks Ralph who is 'boss'. What is Jack's response when Ralph replies that he, Ralph, is boss? What do you think makes Jack change his mind?

In the second last paragraph of the story, we read: 'Ralph wept for the end of innocence, the darkness of man's heart, and the fall through the air of the true, wise friend called Piggy.' Consider each of these three griefs in turn. Now jot down what you think 'the end of innocence' means for Ralph and why he mourns it. Next jot down what 'the darkness of man's heart' means for him and why it makes him cry. Now jot down what you think Ralph's full and final evaluation of Piggy must be.

Imagine you are Jack. Write down your reactions to being rescued. Now imagine you are Roger and write down how you feel about the rescue.

Out of all the boys on the beach, who do you think is most grateful to be rescued and who do you think is least grateful? Why do you think so? Do you think all the boys, in one way or another, will welcome the chance to be 'civilized' again and to have to be guided by the authority of adults? Why do you think so?

We have now read through the whole story. It will be helpful to try to bring together all the things you will have noticed and written about during the second half of the story. To make this easier, take a fresh section of your notebook and on separate pages make the following headings:

(1) Main events
(2) Main characters
(3) Main ideas
(4) Main judgements

(1) MAIN EVENTS

Imagine you are one of the boys who has just been rescued. Do not choose one of the main characters, but imagine you are someone whose name has not been mentioned at all. Now imagine you are on the ship which is taking you all back home. You have been washed, you have eaten and slept and are now ready to tell what has happened. One of the ship's crew asks you what you all did on the island. Now write down all the main events, in the order in which they happened, starting from the seventh chapter.

(2) MAIN CHARACTERS

On this page (you may take extra pages if you wish), set out what each main character is like, as you read onwards from the seventh chapter. Remember to include any changes in appearance which take place after the first half of the story; and to include what the character's interests are and what the others think of him. Include, too, what you think of him. Finally, you may add any thoughts you have about how the character has developed and whether you like the changes, or not.

(3) MAIN IDEAS

Set out here *what* you think the writer has pointed out in the second half of the story. Remember to think about *how* he tells the story. Are there, for example, more significant events in the second half of the story than there were in the first? Why do you think so? The deaths of Simon and Piggy, for example, are obviously significant. Look again at these passages. But there are other important events too. The conversations Simon and Ralph have, for instance, with the 'Lord of the Flies' tell us important things about the writer's point of view. The passage describing the impending storm which comes before the killing of Simon is important too. In such passages, look at how the words are used. Do they, for example, only give information? What other ways are there in which the words are used?

Look again at the notes you made about the main ideas when you were half-way through the story. Remind yourself about the symbols and images you noticed then. Now consider how these symbols and images are developed in the second half of the story. The conch, for example, is smashed to pieces at the same time as Piggy falls to his death. What does the smashing of the conch represent? The fire that sweeps the island at the end of the story is one of many fires throughout the book; but this final fire is what makes the rescue of the boys possible.

As you did earlier, consider as well the arguments the boys have. What points are made? How does the writer make us aware of what his own viewpoint is? Make sure you consider your own viewpoint, after thinking about that of each of the main characters and that of the writer.

(4) MAIN JUDGEMENTS

On this page, continue the diary you began when you thought about the first half of the story. Tell yourself what you think of the concluding half of the story. Remember to include any places where you would have made something different happen or made someone say different things from what they really said. Make sure you write down whether you think the writer did a good job telling his story, or a poor job; as well as whether you think it was a good story and whether you think it was worth telling. Decide, too, whether you would recommend the story for others to read and why.

Characters

Simon, Piggy, Jack and Ralph are the four boys who stand out as the main characters in this story. Others, such as Roger, Sam and Eric, play important parts; but what they do depends a great deal on what one or more of the main four do. That is one way of telling who is a 'main character' in a story: seeing whose thoughts and actions are the most independent, or the least influenced by someone else's thoughts and actions.

Let's look one by one at the main four, beginning with Simon.

SIMON

In an early conflict between Ralph and Jack, Ralph praises Simon for going on helping to build the huts when the others lose interest and go off to play (p. 59). Simon is reliable. But Ralph adds to this assessment the comment: 'He's queer. He's funny.'

One 'queer' thing about Simon is his heading off into the jungle alone. This makes him different from the other boys, none of whom shows the same wish. Jack goes alone to hunt, driven by his obsession, but he is only too happy to have others join him. Simon, on the other hand, makes sure he will not be joined. Read again pages 60–62 and page 146. You will see that Simon has no special activity to pursue – such as hunting or checking the fire – he simply wants to be aware of what is around him. This kind of contemplation and meditation is the basis for the insights he has about the nature of the 'beast'.

Unfortunately for the others, Simon is not good at communicating what he knows and thinks. Read again pages 97–8 and page 113. Simon realizes that he must tell the others that the 'beast' is not an external monster, but a set of emotions inside themselves. What is clear, though, is that he is unable to assert himself above their derision and primitive emotions.

Remember, too, that it is Simon who reassures Ralph – accurately, as it turns out – that Ralph will survive and return to his old life (p. 122). Ralph's response is to tell Simon that he is 'batty', just as earlier on he had decided Simon was 'queer'.

Read pages 151–2 again. Here Simon and the 'Lord of the Flies' – the dead pig's head – seem to have a discussion. Since the pig's head is indeed dead, we know that the thoughts and insights expressed are all Simon's and come to him as insights may come to someone in a dream or a trance. Some of Simon's 'queerness' is accounted for by his tendency to have fits. Epileptics and others who experience fits and trances have long been thought to gain special knowledge during these states and to be more sensitive than most people are in perceiving what is really at the heart of human experiences.

Simon, like Piggy, must submit in the end to the violence and brutality of the others. In a way, like Piggy, Simon knows that death may be his fate, since the 'beast' is the human capacity for destructive passion.

You need to write down your own view of Simon's personality, making sure you list his strengths and weaknesses. You can do so in a series of four to six paragraphs in which you describe Simon both from the inside and from the outside; imagine, for example, that you are Simon trembling at the prospect of speaking in a meeting; and then imagine you are one of the others trying to understand what Simon is saying. When you have written your paragraphs, list the incidents you can remember in which Simon appears most vividly. Next, list what you most like about Simon and then what you do not like or find difficult to understand. Jot down as well whether you have ever known anyone like Simon. Would you like to know someone like Simon better? Why is that?

Finally, think about Simon's death. How far do you think he was responsible for what happened to him? Can you think of anything he could have done differently so that he might have survived? Jot down why you think so.

Imagine now that Simon has survived. He has gone back to his old life, but he hardly ever talks to anybody. Now imagine that you are

Simon, writing his diary. On one or more pages, write down Simon's view of what happened on the island.

PIGGY

You will remember that we meet Piggy right at the beginning of the story, in the first chapter. Jot down briefly the first impressions you had of him. Now jot down your final impression of him, after he has been killed. Next, read your two sets of impressions and see how your views may have changed during the course of the story. Piggy, most of all out of the whole group of boys, is the character about whom we most change our minds. Ralph, too, changes his mind completely about Piggy.

You will have noticed how consistent Piggy is, by contrast. He does not change his mind much about anything. His respect for the conch and its function, for example, remains constant; he dies with the conch in his hands and both he and the shell are smashed to pieces together.

Piggy always explains the lack of reasonableness in the others by saying that they are 'like kids' (pp. 42, 50 and 199). What does he mean? They are all, in any case, children, not adults. How do you think Piggy sees himself (and Ralph) if he says the others are being 'kids'?

Through Ralph's changing attitudes towards Piggy we can trace our own. Read pages 70, 85 and 223 again. Now imagine you are Ralph. Write, on one page or more, an outline of the incidents and reactions that make Ralph change his mind about Piggy.

Next, imagine you are Piggy. On one page or more, write down first why Piggy likes and admires Ralph so much and then what Piggy thinks of Jack and why Jack frightens him.

Main characters in stories are like different voices telling us different points of view about the same things. If Simon has the voice of a visionary who sees into the heart of things, Piggy has the voice of reason, of common sense, of adult ordinariness and safe systems of survival. What do you think of Piggy's kind of common sense? Do you know anyone like Piggy? If so, do you like him or her? Why is that? If you do not know anyone like Piggy, would you like to? Why is that?

What difference do you think Piggy's physical characteristics make to the perceptions of him that the other boys (and we readers) have?

Remember that he is fat and that he suffers from asthma. When one person in a group is physically different from the others, we often make cruel fun of him or her. Why do you think we do that? Jot down why you think so. How do you suggest we could learn better not to have these sorts of reactions to someone who looks different? How far do you think ridiculing Piggy because he looks different and because his asthma prevents him from joining in physical exertion, stops the others from hearing what he has to say? Jot down your view.

Now list the incidents in which you remember Piggy appearing most vividly. Notice whether in each incident Piggy influences the others or is victimized by them. Next, list the things you end up liking about Piggy and then the things you do not like.

Finally, think about Piggy's death. How far do you think he contributed to what happened to him? Could he have done anything differently and so ended up surviving? Imagine Piggy has survived. Now write a page or more of a letter from Piggy to his auntie, in which Piggy tells his own version of what happened on the island.

Now think about Simon and Piggy together. Both are killed at the hands of the others. Do you think they have something in common which would help explain why both of them end up dead? Might it have something to do with their being the only two who see clearly that there is no external 'beast' and that it is the emotions within human beings that are really frightening? Even Ralph wavers and is undecided whether there is a real 'beast' or not. Jack knows that getting everyone else to believe in the 'beast' is essential to his hold over the group; and he knows, too, that he will never be able to get Piggy to believe him and follow him. If Jack and his point of view are to succeed, both Simon and Piggy have to be silenced. Looking at it the other way round, we see that if Simon's and Piggy's point of view is to succeed, they must be able to persuade the others; but we have seen that neither is able to do so. How much do you think this inability is Simon's or Piggy's fault, and how much is it the fault of the others, who simply reject someone who seems 'different'? Jot down why you think so.

JACK

Without Jack, the whole story would be quite different. Here is another way, then, of telling who is a main character in a story: by seeing how someone's presence and actions have tremendous results for everyone else.

Read pages 20–22 again. Here is Jack's first appearance. Is there anything alarming about him? Perhaps not. But there is something striking about him. Despite the horrible experience of being in an aeroplane crash, despite the heat, despite the unfamiliar surroundings and the absence of adults, Jack Merridew has maintained his position as leader of the choir and is exerting a strict discipline over the other choir members.

Jack quickly becomes obsessed with hunting: with tracking, killing, making rituals and being a tribal chief. He becomes obsessed with what Ralph calls being a 'savage'. Read again pages 52–3, where we see this obsession taking root. What makes Ralph and the others take Jack so seriously? Why do you think they do not laugh at him and say, with Piggy, that he's like a 'kid'? Why do you think the choir members, initially, and then gradually nearly all the others, accept Jack's leadership? Jot down your reasons for thinking so.

Read page 69 again. Here Jack first experiments with looking like a 'savage'. (Ralph, by contrast, worries increasingly about his dirty and tattered clothing and hair.) Jot down why you think appearance plays such an important part in Jack's quest for power and for being a successful hunter.

Now think about the relationship between Jack and Ralph. In the beginning they are friends (p. 43). But Jack is resentful that Ralph, rather than himself, is chief. By the middle of the story, Ralph is beginning to realize that Jack sees him as a rival (p. 130). When he has moved away from the beach and established his own tribe, Jack begins to enjoy having the power and authority he has wanted all along and which he has challenged Ralph to gain (p. 165). Notice how the development of Jack's blood-lust and need to hunt and kill parallels the development of his estrangement from Ralph and his growing desire to defeat Ralph and seize Ralph's position as Chief. Think about these developments from Jack's point of view. Now imagine you are Jack and on one page write down how Jack's opinion of Ralph – and his feelings towards Ralph – change between the time of their first meeting to the time of the final hunt. Now take another page and write down Jack's feelings towards Piggy. You will notice that these change much less than do Jack's feelings towards Ralph.

Part of Jack's obsession with power includes establishing rituals. Read pages 149–51 again. Jot down how Jack feels during the dancing and chanting. Now jot down why you think the others respond to Jack's rituals.

Jack does not directly kill Simon or Piggy, but we know he is responsible for their deaths and that by the end he wants Ralph dead too. Write down on one page your own view of what exactly makes Jack responsible and how we know. Now list the most important incidents you remember in which Jack appears most vividly. Then list first the things you like about Jack and next the things you dislike. Have you ever known anyone like Jack? Would you like to? Jot down why you think so.

Finally, imagine you are Jack back at school again and intent upon writing a diary. Now write, on one or more pages, Jack's account of what happened on the island. Is he pleased or resentful about having been rescued? What does he feel about the deaths of Simon and Piggy? Is Jack different at school after his experiences on the island?

RALPH

Ralph is the most important character in the story, because his is the 'central consciousness', in the sense that we see nearly everything that happens through his eyes and feel nearly everything that happens through his feelings.

Jot down what sort of person Ralph is when we first meet him in the opening chapter. Now jot down what he is like at the end. How much do you think he changes as a result of his experiences on the island?

Why do the others respect Ralph and select him as chief when they only laugh at Piggy? Ralph wants to keep the fire going and he wants to be rescued; but he can also be irresponsible and act like a 'kid'. Jot down two or three incidents you remember in which Ralph abandons common sense and behaves like a 'kid'.

Unlike any other character, Ralph is liked by everyone else to start with. Jot down why you think Jack likes him; why you think Piggy likes him; and why you think Simon likes him. Now write down whether you like him or not and why. Next, list the things you dislike about Ralph.

Now read pages 75–80 again. Write on one page or more how Ralph feels when he finds the fire has died out and when Jack boasts about killing the pig. Remember to include how you think Ralph re-asserts his leadership.

Immediately following this incident, Ralph decides that he must call a serious meeting. What is it that Ralph understands and the others do not, which makes him feel that a meeting is urgently needed? Simon sees into the heart of things but cannot communicate what he knows; Piggy can think things out but is always ridiculed; Jack is set upon a quite different path, driven by his obsession with power and killing. Ralph is the only one the others will listen to. And yet he fails, in the end, to persuade them to his point of view. Read pages 83–92 again. Can you notice anything Ralph might have said or done differently, which could have persuaded everyone to agree with him? Do you think, for example, that he could have agreed more openly with Piggy and Simon about the 'beast'?

Think about the deaths of Simon and Piggy. How responsible is Ralph for these deaths? Jot down why you think so. Something is wrong with Ralph's leadership that contributes to Jack's increasing power over the others. What do you think he might lack? Or if you think he does not lack any qualities essential for good leadership, what mistakes do you think he makes? Try to link what you say to incidents you remember in which Ralph appears most vividly.

Now imagine you are Ralph and write down on one or more pages Ralph's opinion of the others and how he feels about them. Remember to include how his perceptions and feelings change, especially towards Piggy and Jack. First write down Ralph's view of Simon; then his view of Piggy; and finally his view of Jack.

Ralph is the character who is most consistently preoccupied with being rescued. Now imagine you are Ralph after the rescue, recovering back home in the country. He has decided to write a letter to the head-teacher of Jack's school in order to explain as best he can why someone should watch Jack carefully. Write the letter, imagining you are Ralph, and describe as exactly as you can what happened on the island. Remember to include how your feelings towards Jack changed.

Now jot down what you think Ralph's thoughts and feelings are as he remembers the deaths of Simon and Piggy. Is Ralph wiser after the rescue than he was before being stranded on the island? Why do you think so?

Now write, on one or more pages, your own opinion about whether it is essential to this story that both the main characters and all the minor ones are boys. If you imagine a group of girls stranded on the island, under the same circumstances, do you think things would happen in the same way? Can you imagine a female Simon, Piggy, Jack and Ralph? Make clear why you have the opinion you do; and whether, therefore, you think the human behaviour we see illustrated in this story is something believable about either boys or girls, men or women, or whether you think only boys, or only boys and men, would follow the pattern of actions and reactions that we have been thinking about as we have been reading this story.

OTHER CHARACTERS

Think for a while about the less important characters and what they are like. Sam and Eric, for example, stay with Ralph almost to the end; and then they betray him. Can you understand why they do? Have you been betrayed by a friend? How did you feel about it? Can you understand your friends if they suddenly 'drop' you?

Roger, more than the others, succeeds in breaking out from the taboo of civilization against murder. What do you think it is in his personality that enables this to happen? Do you know anyone who reminds you of Roger? What might be some special characteristics of such a person?

Think about the differences between Sam and Eric, on the one hand, and Roger, on the other. Where do you think such differences come from? Do you think people are just born the way they are? Or do you think we develop such marked differences from one another as a result of our experiences and the things we learn? Jot down on one page which view you hold and give your reasons for thinking so.

Think about the people you know well, your friends, the members of your family, your teachers and anyone else who is important in your life. Think about how you might describe each of them and about the differences between them. Now think again about the characters in this story. Is there a type of person you know whose character is completely different from any of the boys in the story? Could Golding have used such a character? What sort of difference might it make to how the story turns out? Or do you think whatever combinations of characters the author might have used, the events in the story would have happened anyway, because 'human nature' is the same in any group? Jot down which you think and give your reasons.

Themes

Golding tells us his story in order to encourage us to think about the way people are and to let us see what he finds fascinating and important about human experience. Part of what we do as readers is examine how much we see what he sees and agree with what he thinks about it, and how much we see things differently and come, therefore, to different conclusions about how people are.

CIVILIZATION

In this story, a group of English schoolboys gradually turn into a tribe of 'savages'. We see a process in which the veneer of civilization is slowly stripped away until only the most primitive of human energies – fear and violence or what Golding calls the capacity for evil – are left. This point of view suggests that these energies constitute our most basic nature and that efforts to control this nature are less basic and are more learned. Golding's story illustrates the idea that if we were allowed to do exactly what we liked, almost all of us would end up being 'savages', and that it is only the forced control of civilization that keeps us in check.

Let's look, then, at how Golding suggests the marks of the civilized person as represented by Ralph and Piggy. There is, for example, the regular daily pattern of work, play and eating (p. 64), a pattern which is not natural, but learned. There are the habits of washing, trimming hair, cleaning teeth and nails, dressing tidily and generally keeping up appearances (pp. 120–21). There is that restraint we learn as children which stops us hitting and hurting and bullying other people for our own pleasure (p. 67). In their regression to 'savagery', Jack, Roger and the others reject these behaviours and reject, too, the control of fear and violence which the behaviours stand for.

Neither Ralph nor Piggy really understands why Jack and the others want 'savagery'. Ralph asks Piggy, 'What makes things break up like they do?' (p. 154), but Piggy is only able to answer that it must be Jack, somehow. He means that it must have something to do with Jack's particular nature and personality. Only Simon, in his imagined discussion with the dead pig's head, understands the danger of the forces for violence which people carry within them.

Ralph consistently wants to get back to civilization and sees the maintaining of their fire as the only hope of rescue. But he comes to understand something else about the function of the fire: it is to be a 'hearth' and a 'comfort' (p. 179) which can protect them all from their own fears and imaginings which threaten to break out into the open as violence.

By the end, 'savagery' triumphs and civilization is defeated on the island. Rescue comes at the very end only from the outside world, not from within the group of boys. Think about this. Do you believe the story? Would any group of boys – or girls – actually behave like this? Or is it just this particular group? Is it just a particular kind of personality – Jack's, for example – which makes the regression to 'savagery' inevitable? Write down on one or more pages your own view of whether or not the events of this story depend on particular personalities; or whether you think civilization must always be defeated by 'savagery' in the end.

POWER

One central way in which Golding suggests how civilization can be threatened and made to break down is by illustrating how power can be gained and challenged. The power struggle between Ralph and Jack is the clearest depiction of this process. Ralph, you will remember, was chosen to be chief by the others. He was chosen 'democratically', which means that no one forced the group to choose him, nor did he somehow himself manage to force them to do so. That is both a strength and a weakness of 'democracy': the strength is that people are free to choose and do not have a choice thrust upon them, but the weakness is that they may make the wrong choice. In this story, for example, the group chooses Ralph without really knowing him; perhaps only because they all like him, or perhaps only because they do not want to choose Jack.

Think for a moment about whether the story would have been the same, or quite different, if the others had *chosen* Jack, rather than Ralph, to be chief. If that had happened, Jack would not have had to defeat Ralph's authority in order to set up his tribe. Write down your own view of what you think would have happened if Jack had been chosen as chief right from the beginning.

In the story, the symbol for 'democracy', for ruling by free choice and common sense, is the conch. The shell quickly becomes the authority by which official meetings are called and by which any member of the meeting – from highest to lowest – gains an equal right to speak. Read again pages 49, 111 and 189. You will see how reverently Piggy behaves towards the conch; not because of what it is like – not because it is a beautiful and extraordinary shell – but because of what it stands for: the right to speak and, by speaking, to be able to appeal to the agreement of the group. Jack, by contrast, has contempt rather than reverence for what the conch represents. Read page 166 again. Here Jack tells Piggy that 'the conch doesn't count' at this end of the island. The power Jack respects and craves is not the power of agreement, but the power won by force, by the strongest; and the power which is maintained by encouraging fear of the strongest in others.

The most persuasive element in Jack's perception of power – ruling by strength and fear – is the threat of death. Jack's passion for hunting the pig, for spilling blood, for killing, is only partly explained by his insistence that they all need fresh meat to eat. It quickly becomes clear that for him, killing is an end in itself; and that, to the killer, killing gives a greater sense of power than does anything else. Killing gives what Golding calls the knowledge 'that they had outwitted a living thing, imposed their will upon it, taken away its life like a long satisfying drink' (p. 76).

Inevitably, it seems, killing pigs begins to be an insufficient way of satisfying Jack's need for power. People are to be next; and Simon, the first such victim, is killed in the ritual which celebrates the slaying of pigs. Ralph, when he is finally on the run, knows that he will suffer the same fate, because the 'painted savages would go further and further'

(p. 203). Power gained by force and fear must be maintained by force and fear.

LORD OF THE FLIES

At the centre of a rule by force, Golding suggests, is the necessity for superstition and magic. Fear of ordinary strength is not enough, because sooner or later a stronger force can be mounted against it. If the others ganged up against Jack and Roger, for example, the two fierce boys – however strong and frightening they were – would be outnumbered and defeated. That would be a reasonable or common-sense approach to a threatening strength or fear; and it is the approach Simon shows us when he walks right up to the flapping figure on the mountain-top and sees it for what it is: a dead parachutist.

Piggy, like Simon, knows that the only things to fear are the forces within human beings. You will remember that Piggy's way of expressing this same knowledge is to say that life is 'scientific'. Unfortunately for everyone, Ralph – the chief – is not so sure and succumbs sometimes to a fear of the 'beast'.

Now read pages 151–2 again. The dead pig's head – staked by Jack to be a superstitious offering to the 'beast' – reminds Simon that what is happening is a 'bad business'. Flies, attracted to the rotting flesh, feast upon it as the boys have begun feasting upon roast meat and upon the acts of hunting and killing. 'Fancy thinking the Beast was something you could hunt and kill,' Simon realizes. Later, when Ralph comes across the staked head, it fills him with rage and loathing and he smashes it to pieces (p. 204). By the end of the story, then, both the conch – symbol of ruling by reason and agreement – and the 'Lord of the Flies' – symbol of ruling by killing and superstitious fear – are destroyed. But there is an essential difference between these two symbols and what they stand for. The shell exists in nature; its form and properties are beautiful in themselves. The staked head, by contrast, has been wrested from life by an act of human violence; it has become horrible and horrifying. Ralph – and particularly Piggy – genuinely believe in the right to choose and to speak which the conch is taken to represent; whereas Jack himself does not believe in the 'beast', but makes sure that the rest of his tribe does. Jack uses the initial fears of the others in order to build up his own power.

We can see now that Golding wants his story to tell us something about what groups of human beings can be like anywhere, at any time; and what things we need to be aware of if we do not want to fall back into what he calls 'savagery'. Now that you have read the story carefully, you need to decide what you think of it and whether you agree with Golding's picture of what we are really like. Jot down, therefore, any incidents or experiences you know of in which people's fears are whipped up into a superstitious fear of a 'beast'. Wartime is one obvious example. Those on the other side become the enemy and ultimately become not people at all, but become an idea of evil which we are encouraged to hate and destroy. For some people at present, to take another example, the idea of 'communism' is a kind of 'beast' which must be hunted and destroyed. On a much smaller scale, in your class or family or neighbourhood, you may be aware of how a 'beast' has been created by a small group of human beings, in order to fend off some fear or threat and to help the people in the group to feel more secure and powerful. Sometimes the 'beast' is a person who is different in some way from the rest. When you think about it, you will find there are a great many examples of 'beasts' all around you. Jot down some examples of your own; and make sure you add who you think made the 'beast' and how the group's fear of it is maintained.

During the time in which you are reading and studying this story, notice how actual stories from life are written about in newspapers and magazines. Cut out three or four and read them carefully, trying to see how your 'shock' and 'horror' as a reader are encouraged by the way the story is written. You will find, for example, that a prostitute or a homosexual or a foreigner can often be presented as a 'beast'; whereas others who are thought 'normal' are often written about sympathetically. This process of making 'scapegoats' and of making sterotypes is part of how superstitions are created and maintained. (Look up the word 'scapegoat' in your dictionary and think of the number of ways in which you might use this word to explain how the groups you know of behave.) Part of Golding's point of view is the warning in his story that unless we are aware of our capacity to join in, we are in danger of reacting in the same ways Jack's followers do.

One problem most of the boys have with Ralph's nagging about the fire and with Piggy's insistence on common sense and not being like 'kids', is that it is no fun. The things Ralph and Piggy want soon seem dull and boring. There seems to be nothing exciting about being reasonable and sensible. It is obvious to most of the boys that it is much more fun and much more exciting to go hunting and to have rituals and feasts. Being cruel and primitive seems more attractive than being civilized. How much do you agree with this reaction? Do you think what Jack offers is more fun and more attractive? Jot down why you think so. Now write down what things Ralph or Piggy might have thought of to make being civilized more fun for the others.

Imagine now that you have charge of all the boys on the island. Write down what you might suggest everyone can do, making sure that you can maintain the sensible things that are necessary, like keeping the fire going and building the shelters, while at the same time making sure that there is enough fun for everyone. Write down your suggestions in the form of a programme, perhaps by dividing up the hours in the day for different tasks and activities. (You will remember that clocks and watches are unnecessary, since Golding describes how the boys know the different times of the day from the movement of the sun and the changes in light and heat.) Now write down some more particular suggestions. What might Jack do? What might Roger specially do? How could Simon be encouraged to talk more in meetings and the others be encouraged to listen to him? What could Piggy do so that the others, not only Ralph, could see his good qualities and make friends with him? Can being civilized be more fun?

You may think that Golding's story is so likely and so believable – even so inevitable – that nothing anyone might try or suggest could change the result. In that case, write down, on one or more pages, what you think makes the result inevitable. Is it particular personalities which cannot change and which – unless forced to stop – will always seek to spill blood and to rule by terror? Or is it the combination of particular personalities locked into a struggle for power, fuelled by the weakness of the rest of the group in its desire to be led: to have a leader at any cost, irrespective of what kind of leadership it is? Or do you have a different idea of what might make such a result inevitable?

One question Golding's story leads us to is the question of who is responsible. When 'savagery' happens amongst us – when, for example, someone is raped, mugged, murdered or victimized in any way – to what extent are we all responsible? Or to what extent do you think leaders and people in authority are responsible? Was what happened on the island Jack's responsibility? Or Ralph's? Or was it the shared responsibility of the whole group? Write down on one or more pages what your view is and why.

INNOCENCE

The final image in the story is that of Ralph weeping on the beach, together with the little boys, who are also weeping, and the officer, who is both moved and embarrassed by this display of grief. We are told that Ralph weeps for the loss of innocence, the darkness of man's heart and the death of Piggy.

Innocence is often thought of as a lack of guilt or a lack of sin; but it means as well a lack of knowledge. The officer has said to Ralph that he would have thought a group of British boys – meaning civilized boys – would have put up a 'better show'. (Piggy would have expressed it by saying they ought to have done better than to behave like 'kids'.) Ralph replies that they had begun all right, when they were 'together'. The officer has assumed – as Ralph did at the beginning – that acting reasonably and being civilized would come naturally.

Ralph's loss of innocence is in part his new knowledge that he can never make that assumption again. He knows things he did not know before; that 'the darkness of man's heart' is a capacity for evil so deeply rooted that civilization can only triumph over it with a constant effort of human will and intelligence. Reasonableness and civilized actions cannot be taken for granted, but must be planned and insisted upon if people are not to revert to 'savagery'.

The suggestion is that 'savagery' is our natural state and that civilization is our effort to rise above it; to find ways of suppressing our instincts for power, for killing, for being led, for believing in 'beasts'.

You must come to your own conclusion about whether your view is the same as Golding's. There are many 'savages', in many cultures around the world, who do not spend their energies killing each other and burning up islands. To see civilization – British or any other kind – as a superior way of conquering the 'darkness' in us is to begin to make the mistake of thinking 'we' are not like 'them', we are not evil and destructive, we would not behave like the boys on the island.

What is more interesting and useful to think about is that struggles for power take place in any group and that victims suffer in any group, whether the group is civilized or not. Simon, after all, is not innocent of this knowledge in the way Ralph is at the beginning; and Piggy, Ralph concludes at the very end, was 'wise': he knew what the dangers were and where they lay.

One result of the ending of innocence is the taking of responsibility for what happens around us; it is to 'grow up', and not be 'kids' any longer. Whether Jack ever 'grows up' is left unclear; Ralph, on the other hand, is forced to. Think for a while about whether this story has made you 'grow up' at all.

Passages for Comparison

The following story was printed in the *Observer*, London, on 28 October 1984:

'Mother pleads for English boy on Death Row'
from Ben Barber in Miami

The mother of a 17-year-old English youth facing a death sentence on a charge of murder in Florida is appealing to the Foreign Office in an effort to seek his extradition.

David Gottfried goes on trial on 5 November, accused, with an American youth, of murdering his 10-year-old step-sister Karla in Miami. Mrs Carol Gottfried and her lawyer want him to be tried in Britain, which is possible under British law ...

From his cell in the Dade County jail last week, Gottfried spoke of his hopes of going home. 'I'd like to go on a plane and get back to England,' he said. He is charged with murdering his step-sister on 26 January. The girl was stabbed more than a dozen times with a knife and shot once in the head.

The co-defendant, Gottfried's flat-mate Nelson Molina, 21, is claiming insanity due to 'television intoxication', the same defence used by his lawyer, Ellis Rubin, in 1977 in defending 15-year-old Ronnie Zamora. Rubin claimed then that his client had spent an excessive amount of time watching violent police series on television, including *Kojak* and *Baretta*. Zamora was sentenced to life imprisonment for killing an 82-year-old woman.

If Gottfried is found guilty of first degree murder he faces life in prison or death in the electric chair. He admits he's 'upset – it's not too good'.

He lived with his divorced mother in Abbey Wood, south-east London, until he went to his father, also called David, in Miami Beach three years ago. The boy attended a local junior high school but after his father remarried, he dropped out of school and took jobs at a travel agency and cleaning up in a restaurant. He also moved out of his father's flat to one shared with Molina and their girlfriends. His father disappeared after his son's arrest.

Police claim young Gottfried confessed to his step-sister's murder and gave them a 53-page statement. Nevertheless, he pleads not guilty ...

The following extract is taken from Timothy Findlay, *Famous Last Words* (Penguin, Toronto, 1981), pp. 165–7

All that afternoon I sat with Isabella in the blacksmith's yard on a bench beneath the vine. The walls of the yard and the building around us were white and the vine's new leaves were rainy green. The air was filled with the smell of olive wood and smoke and sun-hot stones. A woman came and brought us wine and bread and pears. The pears were dry and small, but very sweet.

Isabella sat with her legs straight out and crossed at the ankles, showing bruises on her shins I had not been aware existed. These were doubtless from the bombing raid on the road, but, combined with the haunted expression in her eyes, the effect was of a torture victim sitting incongruous in the sun.

Isabella said, 'They took him from his office into a courtyard such as this – with vines and trees ...'

This was a complete *non sequitur*.

'What?' I said.

But Isabella hardly seemed to know I was there. She was sitting somewhere else, I suppose; in the past.

'My husband was only thirty-eight years old,' she said, 'and all he had done was express his opinion. All he had done was put some words on paper. But they killed him – shot him – propping him up against the courtyard wall – and they placed the gun in his hands, and they laid my children, all of them dead, around him. As if he had killed them.' She was peering through the heat, as if to see the scene she described.

I waited.

In a moment she spoke again. 'When our friend Matteotti died, he was beaten first. With stones. Were you aware of that?'

'No.' I had only known he was shot, and told her so. I was watching her carefully. She was perspiring; running a fever; ill – and the words were coming out of dreams ... She opened her eyes. 'These men – Matteotti and my husband – were writers. Only writers, my friend. Only men of words ...' And she looked at me, informing me of something that I did not know, perhaps about the dangers of writing.

And I did not. Know.

'My husband was a poet. Just a poet ...' She looked at the wall. 'But Mussolini's people took him into a courtyard. Under the trees ...' She spoke as if the trees had been disgraced. 'And they killed him. You see? Our friends, my friend. *Our friends.* They killed him.' Reaching down, she drew her skirt across the bruises on her shins. 'And now, in Spain, I am constantly thinking of my husband and his death,' she said. 'How they killed him. With their boots.

And I am thinking all the time of Matteotti, too; and how they killed him. With a stone. And I am thinking of my children . . . I am thinking of the wall and of the trees. I am thinking of human beings. I am thinking of how it can be that mere human beings can be so afraid of the written word that they will kill to be rid of it. In a courtyard such as this. On a day such as this – with the vines and the trees and the stones as their witness. How can that be?' she asked me. 'Tell me. Tell me. How can that be?'

I did not know.

'And now,' she said, 'we are here in Spain. Twelve years have passed – and we are here in Spain and the stones and boots that killed Matteotti and my husband, the bullets that killed my children, have become the bombs on that road and the shells from the ships offshore. And nothing is for the better. Nothing is changed for the better. Everything of which we dreamed is gone and all that we feared would happen has come to be. Are you afraid, my friend? Are you never afraid of what we do? Of the meaning of what we do and who we are?'

The first of these extracts is a piece of news journalism printed in a newspaper; the second is a piece of prose fiction, an extract from a story, just as *Lord of the Flies* is a story. The first is true, in the sense that it reports actual people and actual happenings; the second is a truthful view of the possibilities of human nature. In each extract, the victims who are murdered are well-known to their murderers, just as Simon and Piggy were well-known to the other boys on the island. What do you think were the reasons for David Gottfried and Nelson Molina to kill the ten-year-old girl who was David Gottfried's step-sister? To what extent do you believe watching violent series on television has anything to do with the reasons?

What 'beast' might the two young men try to say they were killing? In the second piece, Fascist friends kill two poets. The wife of one of them, reflecting twelve years later to a friend, suggests that the 'beast' these people were trying to kill was 'the written word'. She finds herself unable to understand in any way how words can have provoked these murders, together with the murders of her children.

After you have read these extracts again and thought about them from the point of view of an onlooker or observer, take your notebook and write a story of your own. In your story, include a victim who is well-known to his or her murderer and an observer – who may be yourself or who may be someone else – who is trying to understand the reasons why the murderer needs to kill. When you have worked out these requirements, include as well the conclusions the observer comes to about what must now happen to the murderer: how he or she can be made to understand what the observer understands.

When you are satisfied with your story, exchange it with someone else's story; or with more than one other person's if you are working together in a group. Read as many other stories as you can. Then discuss your own and the other stories together, so that you can note down what further things you have learned about 'the darkness of man's heart' and what may be done about it.

You may find a dominant theme in your own or other stories, in which the observer feels a need to punish the murderer. Try not to dwell too much on this possibility. Try, instead, to think about what changes in conditions, or in education or in other ways we influence one another need to be undertaken if we are to develop in a manner which will prevent the need to kill one another.

Glossary

Here are listed alphabetically some of the more unusual words used by Golding in *Lord of the Flies*. If there are other words in the text whose meaning you are unclear about, make sure you look up their precise meanings in your dictionary.

The meanings given here have been chosen as much as possible to help clarify the uses of the words in the story; but there are times when Golding uses a word figuratively or metaphorically, so that the meaning given to the word by the dictionary will not exactly explain his particular use of it. One example is his use of the word 'fledged' (p. 10), which literally means 'feathered', but which he uses to give an image of how the palm trees look like feathers against the shore-line of the island. You will notice many other metaphorical uses of words in this story, especially in the descriptive passages.

abdomen: the part of the human body lying between the thorax or chest and the pelvis, where the liver and the gut are found

acrid: sharp or biting to the taste; pungent; bitter

antagonism: opposition

antiphonal: alternate choral singing

apex: the tip, point or summit of anything

aromatic: fragrant; sweet-scented

arrogance: the pride which exalts one's own importance; pride with contempt for others; haughtiness; disdain

asserted: affirmed positively; put forward one's own rights and claims

avidly: eagerly

bastion: a huge mass of earth, faced with sods, bricks or stones, standing out from a fortification

belligerence: a disposition to fighting and warfare

blatant: bellowing; noisy; obtrusive; obvious

bole: the body, stem or trunk of a tree

bourdon: the drone of the bagpipe; a drone-like quality of sound

bow-stave: curved length of timber fitted to the prow end of a boat

chapter chorister: member of the choir of a cathedral chapter (a chapter is a bishop's council)

chastisement: pain inflicted for punishment and correction *cirque:* a kind of circular valley among mountains

clarity: clearness

coign: a corner

conspiratorial: plotting; agreeing to an underhand plan

context: the weaving of several parts into one whole; the relevance of each part of something to each other part

crepitation: sharp crackling sound, or rattle like dried twigs, or salt thrown on a fire

cue: a signal on which to act

cynicism: contempt for the pleasures and arts of life; moroseness; sneering

declivities: slopes; inclinations downward

decorum, decorous: seemliness; decency of speech or behaviour; suitability

delirious: crazy; raving; frenzied

demoniac: pertaining to demons or evil spirits; extremely wicked or cruel

demure: affectedly modest or coy; grave or reserved consciously and intentionally

derisive: mocking; ridiculing

detritus: disintegrated materials of rocks; waste materials

diaphragm: a muscle separating the chest from the abdomen and vital to breathing

diffidently: lacking in trust or confidence

digit: finger

discursive: rambling; argumentative, passing rapidly from one subject to another

dubiety: doubtfulness

ebullience: a boiling-over; an overflow; a bursting-forth

eccentric: deviating or departing from the centre; given to act in a way peculiar to oneself and different from other people

effigy: an image or likeness of a person or thing

efflorescence: bursting into bloom; the time of flowering; eruption

effulgence: a flood of light; great lustre or brightness

elemental: arising from or pertaining to first or primary principles

embossed: covered with protuberances; raised work; work in relief

ensconce: to cover or shelter; protect, hide securely

epaulettes: ornamental shoulder-pieces worn on military and naval uniforms

errant: wandering; rambling

evacuation: making empty; removal of everyone from a building, town or city

festoon: garland with flowers or foliage

fledged: feathered

fluking: winging

foliage: all the leaves of a plant together

fulcrum: prop or support

furtive: stealthy; thief-like

generic: referring to a large group

gesticulate: make gestures

grimace: make a wry face; smirk

grotesque: having a wild, extraordinary or extravagant form; of the utmost oddness

guano: decomposed excrement of seabirds

gyration: a circular motion; a turning or whirling round

hiatus: an opening; a gap

Home Counties: those counties lying close to London: Hertfordshire, Bedfordshire, Buckinghamshire, Surrey, Kent, Essex

hysteria: a nervous affection characterized by fits of laughing and crying; uncontrollable laughter

ill-omened: a casual occurrence thought to predict something evil

immured: confined; enclosed; walled in

impaired: made worse; lessened in quality

impalpable: not able to be felt by touching

impending: hanging over; imminent

impervious: incapable of being passed through; incapable of being made to react

incantation: the act of using certain words and ceremonies for the purpose of performing magical actions; the form of those words; a magical spell

incredulous: not believing things readily

incursion: an invasion; an inroad

induced: led by persuasion or argument

ineffectual: inefficient; weak

inscrutable: incapable of being searched into and understood; not able to be satisfactorily accounted for or explained

interpose: interrupt; interfere

intricate, intricacies: entangled; involved; difficult to follow or unravel; complicated

iridescent: giving out colour; gleaming or shimmering with rainbow colours

irrelevance: the inapplicability of something; its not having any bearing on the point at issue

lagoon: shallow lake or sheet of water connected with the sea or a river; also the sheet of water surrounded by a ring-shaped coral island

legendary: fabulous, as in ancient stories of marvellous characters and events

leviathan: a fabulous sea-monster of immense size

ludicrous: very ridiculous; comical

malevolently: with ill-will; spitefully

martyred: persecuted; tormented

matins: Christian morning worship or service

mirages: natural optical illusions, such as apparent hills, coasts, ships and so on

mortification: humiliation

motif: recurrent image or theme

myopia: short-sightedness

node: a nob; a knot on a stem where leaves grow from

octave: the seven notes of a musical scale plus the first note of the succeeding one

officious: annoyingly eager to oblige or assist; meddling

omission: a neglect or failure to do something that should have been done; the act of leaving something out

opaque: impervious to the rays of light; not transparent

pallor: paleness

pendant: hanging

perpendicular: perfectly upright or vertical

phantoms: spectres; ghosts; fancied visions; unreal things

pliant: capable of being easily bent; readily yielding to force or pressure without breaking

plinth: a flat square or slab

precentor: leader of the choir in a cathedral

proffer: to hold out something so that a person may take it; to offer for acceptance

propitiatingly: appeasingly

purged: cleansed; purified

quota: a proportional part or share

rapt: entirely absorbed

rebuke: to reprimand directly and severely

recrimination: the return of one accusation with another

screes: debris of rocks; shingle; loose stones

sepals: one of the separate divisions of the calyx of a flower where the calyx is made up of various leaves

slewed: turned or swung around

smirking: smiling affectedly or sillily

specious: appearing well at first sight

speculate: consider; reflect; theorize

strident: harsh; grating

suffusion: spreading over

susurration: soft, buzzing, murmuring sound; whispering; rustling

swarthiness: darkness of complexion

swathes, swathing: wrapping; binding as with bandages

taboo: something set apart; something prohibited

tacit: implied but not expressed in words

talisman: a charm consisting of a magical figure, supposed to give protection from evil, injury, disease or sudden death

tendril: a slender, spiral shoot of a plant that winds around another body for support

terrace: a raised level space or platform of earth, supported on one or more sides by a bank of turf

testily: fretfully; peevishly

theological: to do with the study of divine things

theorem: a position laid down as acknowledged by reason or an established principle

tirade: a long, violent speech

torrid: parched; violently hot; burning

tow: the coarse and broken part of flax or hemp

typhoon: violent hurricane

ululation: howling like a dog or wolf

vicissitudes: changes; passing from one state or condition to another

warped: twisted out of shape

wind-breaker: weather-proof jacket similar to an anorak

FOR THE BEST IN PAPERBACKS, LOOK FOR THE

In every corner of the world, on every subject under the sun, Penguin represents quality and variety – the very best in publishing today.

For complete information about books available from Penguin – including Pelicans, Puffins, Peregrines and Penguin Classics – and how to order them, write to us at the appropriate address below. Please note that for copyright reasons the selection of books varies from country to country.

In the United Kingdom: For a complete list of books available from Penguin in the U.K., please write to *Dept E.P., Penguin Books Ltd, Harmondsworth, Middlesex, UB7 0DA*

In the United States: For a complete list of books available from Penguin in the U.S., please write to *Dept BA, Penguin, 299 Murray Hill Parkway, East Rutherford, New Jersey 07073*

In Canada: For a complete list of books available from Penguin in Canada, please write to *Penguin Books Canada Ltd, 2801 John Street, Markham, Ontario L3R 1B4*

In Australia: For a complete list of books available from Penguin in Australia, please write to the *Marketing Department, Penguin Books Australia Ltd, P.O. Box 257, Ringwood, Victoria 3134*

In New Zealand: For a complete list of books available from Penguin in New Zealand, please write to the *Marketing Department, Penguin Books (NZ) Ltd, Private Bag, Takapuna, Auckland 9*

In India: For a complete list of books available from Penguin, please write to *Penguin Overseas Ltd, 706 Eros Apartments, 56 Nehru Place, New Delhi, 110019*

In Holland: For a complete list of books available from Penguin in Holland, please write to *Penguin Books Nederland B.V., Postbus 195, NL–1380 AD Weesp, Netherlands*

In Germany: For a complete list of books available from Penguin, please write to *Penguin Books Ltd, Friedrichstrasse 10 – 12, D–6000 Frankfurt Main 1, Federal Republic of Germany*

In Spain: For a complete list of books available from Penguin in Spain, please write to *Longman Penguin España, Calle San Nicolas 15, E–28013 Madrid, Spain*

FOR THE BEST IN PAPERBACKS, LOOK FOR THE

PENGUIN BOOKS OF POETRY

American Verse
Ballads
British Poetry Since 1945
Caribbean Verse
A Choice of Comic and Curious Verse
Contemporary American Poetry
Contemporary British Poetry
Eighteenth-Century Verse
Elizabethan Verse
English Poetry 1918–60
English Romantic Verse
English Verse
First World War Poetry
Georgian Poetry
Irish Verse
Light Verse
London in Verse
Love Poetry
The Metaphysical Poets
Modern African Poetry
Modern Arab Poetry
New Poetry
Poems of Science
Poetry of the Thirties
Post-War Russian Poetry
Spanish Civil War Verse
Unrespectable Verse
Victorian Verse
Women Poets